PRAISE FOR
VENTURING IN SOUTHERN GREECE

Venturing in Southern Greece is an indispensable guide to the heart of the region. During their travels through the town of Neapoli and villages of Mesochori, Faraklo, Lachi, and others, these writers experienced the great variety and richness of Greek culture on the southern Peloponnese. They recount their adventures in delightful essays. These writers have captured the spirit of Vatika.

—YIANNIS KOUSSOULIS, Mayor of the Municipality of Vatika

These writers came to Vatika to explore this little-known region of Greece. As they visited its villages, swam at its beaches, walked its paths, savored local food and wine, danced, and sang, they not only discovered Vatika, but made personal discoveries as well. Listen carefully to each writer's voice as she examines some specific aspect of this portion of the Peloponnese. Humorous, poignant, lively, or pensive, each piece will add to your understanding and appreciation of southern Greece—and make you wish you could have joined them there.

—MARKOS KOUNALAKIS, publisher of *The Washington Monthly*

What a wonderful opportunity to travel through the eyes of writers who chose the land of the Gods to explore the past and discover the new. We invite you to read about the place that was immortalized by Socrates and revitalized by the 2004 Summer Olympic Games.

—THE ATHENS TOURISM AND ECONOMIC DEVELOPMENT AGENCY

Venturing
in
Southern Greece

The Vatika Odysseys

Edited by Barbara J. Euser & Connie Burke

TRAVELERS' TALES
PALO ALTO

Travelers' Tales and *Traveler' Tales Guides* are trademarks of Travelers' Tales, Inc., 853 Alma Street, Palo Alto, California 94301.

For permission to print essays in this volume, grateful acknowledgement is made to the holders of copyright named on pages 241–250.

Grateful acknowledgement is made to Argonne Hotel Press in Washington, D.C., for permission to reprint "Penelope and the Suitors" by Joanna Biggar.

Front and back cover photographs copyright by Dimitri Delacovias.
Front cover: *Ruins of the fortress above Aghia Paraskevi, overlooking Neapoli and Neapolis Bay, with the low silhouette of the island of Elafonisos in the background.*
Back cover top: *Boats moored on Elafonisos island in the clear waters of Neapolis Bay.*
Back cover bottom: *Panorama of the town of Neapoli.*

Cover design by Sabine Reifig, Menta Design, Athens, Greece.
Interior design by Melanie Haage using the fonts Centaur and Californian.

Distributed by: Publishers Group West, 1700 Fourth Street, Berkeley, California 94710.

CATALOGUING DATA
Venturing in Southern Greece: The Vatika Odysseys/edited by Barbara J. Euser and Connie Burke.

ISBN-10: 1932361456
ISBN-13: 978-1-932361-45-2

1. Greece—Description and travel. 2. Greece—Social life and customs. 3. Peloponnese—Description and travel. 4. Peloponnese—Social life and customs I. Title. II. Euser, Barbara J. III. Burke, Connie

First Edition
Printed in the United States of America
10 9 8 7 6 5 4 3 2 1

To our mothers
Jeannette Virginia Flautz Euser
and the late Chrysanthy "Soula" Leones

Contents

Contents

Preface

Venturing in Southern Greece: The Vatika Odysseys is the product of a writers' workshop held in July 2006 in Mesochori, one of the villages of Vatika, on the southern tip of the Peloponnese. But the idea for the workshop originated in the summer of 2005 in southern France. During a writers' workshop I organized on a boat on the Canal du Midi, Connie Burke, one of the participants, said, "This is great! Let's do it again next summer in Greece."

Connie took charge of organizing the 2006 workshop in Greece. That was only natural. She has lived in Greece for twenty-five years, first as an expatriate American, now as a Greek citizen. She co-edited this volume.

Through Connie I met Virginia, who opened her home to the writers. The instructors for the 2006 workshop, Linda Watanabe McFerrin and Joanna Biggar, had also served as instructors in 2005. Thanasis Maskaleris joined us for an afternoon workshop and evening of dancing. Professor emeritus at San Francisco State College, thirty years ago he taught creative writing to both Connie and Linda.

The circle of people involved in this year's workshop became close friends. You will have a chance to meet all of them in the pages that follow. Each writer's voice is unique. As a group, they blend into a chorus to give a clear picture of Vatika.

The trip to Greece was also an adventure. Several had been to Greece before, but for the rest, it was a new experience. Books and films can offer only a pale facsimile of the land, wind, water, sun, music, and *chara tis zois—joie de vivre*, that we got to know first-hand. Even for those who had been to Greece in the past, Vatika was a new discovery.

We hope you will enjoy your visit to Vatika as you read the essays in this book. It is a place worth visiting. If you cannot travel there in person, these stories are the next best thing to being there.

—Barbara J. Euser

Foreword

"But the places await their interpreters..."
—LAWRENCE DURRELL, *THE SPIRIT OF PLACE*

When my former student, Linda Watanabe McFerrin, asked me to join her and another former student, Connie Burke, and their group of travel writers at the southeastern tip of Peloponnese I said "yes" without knowing what delights were in store for me in their midst.

When I arrived, and met them, their senses were already brimming to ecstasy . . . lucky mortals! They were staying in a beautiful house perched high above Neapoli, in Mesochori, overlooking Neapolis Bay with Elafonisos and Aphrodite's island, Kythira, in spectacular view—a place the immortals would envy, especially if they were received by the group's host, Virginia, native of Neapoli, gifted with all the graces, and Greek *philoxenia* at its best—offerings for the pleasure of guests.

The group was immersed in the surrounding land- and seascapes and, equally, into local life and culture. For days they had been absorbing what they saw and heard—from trees, rocks and traditional architecture to the braying of donkeys, and the ceaseless serenade of summer, orchestrated and performed by the invisible cicadas. I knew then that these women were not ordinary travelers but travelers tuned to write about "the spirit of place."

It was exciting for me—a privileged experience—to witness these new Bacchae at their temporary habitat, at home with Dionysus and Apollo (away from the ravages of excessive technology and artificial matter) moving from enthusiasm (*enthusiasmos* meaning "with the god inside") to ecstasy, transforming themselves under the guidance of both gods, creating their own forms of self, and shaping *logos*—their writing.

In the late afternoon, after my comments on Dionysus given on one of the terraces of the beautiful house, and after the reading of their writing-in-progress, in the still brilliant light of the long Greek day, the slowly-unfolding Greek evening began—all were ready to feast on delicious taverna specialties and eager to join Virginia, now a woman-Zorba, in dance and Dionysian revelry.

These women from California were demonstrating, like other writers/travelers in Greece before them—from Byron to Henry Miller and Lawrence Durrell—that *"Greece offers you something harder: the discovery of yourself."* (Durrell) The Greek revelation was luminously clear on their faces: *anthropos* and Nature in a harmonious synthesis inspiring self-enrichment and endless transformation.

—Thanasis Maskaleris

Illustrations

Through Vineyards and Villages: A Memoir in Progress

CONNIE BURKE

Journal Entry: Wednesday, June 28, 2006

The journey south was long. Luggage, linens, books, towels, cd's, laptops, a cot and five large tins of illy espresso accompanied us to Vatika. The drive from Piraeus seems less arduous considered in four parts: a) one hour from Piraeus to Corinth (in moderate traffic); b) fifty minutes from Corinth to Tripoli; c) forty-five minutes from Tripoli to Sparta; and, d) two hours from Sparta to Neapoli. We stopped for lunch at a roadside taverna in the mountain village of Alepohori, about twenty minutes past Tripoli. Sitting at a wooden table spread with a paper tablecloth held down by a basket of bread, a water jug, two glasses and our cutlery, we relished the tranquility of this mountain sanctuary of

1

ancient oak and pensive plane. We ate in silence, listening to a choir of cicadas singing to the rustle of leaves as a cool mountain breeze passed through the wooden pillars on our roadside porch. Sharing a *choriatiko* (village) salad of tomatoes, cucumbers, onion, and feta cheese, we broke bread with our hands and wiped the juices from our plates.

After eating, we drove over the mountain ridge and down into the Prefecture of Lakonia. The last town we passed before entering the Municipality of Vatika, or Vion, was called Daemonia: that is "Demon" in its feminine form. Dante wrote that if you walked through hell, you could climb your way to paradise. We drove through Daemonia to get to Vatika, a region very close to paradise. Our journey through the vineyards and villages of Vatika had begun.

Vatika, or Vion, is a derivation of *Boiai*, or *Bioatika*. Vatika was beleaguered for centuries by numerous invasions and brutal occupations. From the seventh century B.C. until the mid thirteenth century A.D., Vatika was subjugated in turn by Spartans, Athenians, Romans, and Franks. Its economic and cultural power had declined by the end of the fourth century, following a major earthquake that shook the coastline, submerged part of the major town, and altered the topography of the land. Its bays and coves became havens for pirates.

The Byzantines ruled from the second half of the thirteenth century until the Ottoman Empire invaded Greece in the fifteenth century. For the next three centuries, the Venetians and Ottomans battled to control Vatika. Even after the Venetians signed a peace accord with the Ottoman Empire and agreed to share occupation of Vatika, both sides continued to battle over who would have sole authority of its major port, now known as Neapoli.

In 1821, the Greeks waged a successful war of independence against the Ottoman Empire. Many *Vatikiotes* (men and women from Vatika) took up arms and fought bravely in the mountains of Vatika to secure freedom. After the signing of the Treaty of Constantinople in July 1832, Greece was finally recognized as a sovereign state.

Today, the region of Vatika is noted for its beautiful fishing and mountain villages, waterfront cafes and restaurants, long sandy beaches, mountain springs, archaeological sites, Byzantine churches and fortresses, and Neolithic caves. Vatika is also famous for its onions, its excellent olive oil, and its fishing. It is close to the islands of Kythira and Elafonisos, the medieval town of Monemvasia, and the lovely seaside town of Gytheio.

Journal Entry: Friday, June 30

After a soothing midday swim at Narantzones beach, about two kilometers west of Neapoli near the village of Kambos, we drove to the town square of Neapoli for lunch at a popular taverna called Neapoli. We feasted on half a kilo of freshly caught *barbounia* (red mullet), a plate of spinach, fried potatoes (always fried in olive oil), and a *choriatiko* salad accompanied by half a kilo of white barrel wine. The midday meal is always the main meal of the day, followed by a restful nap and a late afternoon coffee.

In the square near the pier, stands a bronze statue called "The Vatikioti" (man from Vatika). Wearing a fisherman's cap, he gazes at the sandy beaches that stretch out along the bay of the southwestern shore of Neapolis Bay. He stands tall, poised to heave the coiled line in his right hand: a reminder of the significance of the sea to all who visit Vatika and find themselves in her capital, Neapoli.

The ancient city of Boiai (pronounced Vi-e), was founded during the Mycenaean era in the second century B.C. In the second century A.D., Pausanias, a Greek traveler and geographer, wrote that Boiai was founded by King Boios, a descendent of Heracles. Ancient Boiai was populated by inhabitants of three nearby Mycenaean cities, namely Etis, Sidi, and Aphrodisias. Today, it is called Neapoli, meaning "new city." It is the southernmost seaside town of mainland Greece in the Peloponnese.

Neapoli is the governmental, commercial, cultural, and social center of Vatika. In the past it has been called the "Bride of the Lakonian Gulf." While its maritime tradition is still clear, its beaches and seaside cafes, bars, and restaurants make it an attractive holiday destination. Whitewashed houses with ceramic-tiled roofs stretch along Neapolis Bay at the foot of Mt. Parnon. The bay borders the peninsula of Epidaurus Limira, culminating in Cape Maleas.

Journal Entry, July 1
Vatika may be Greece's best-kept secret. Though rich in ancient and Byzantine history, folklore, and agriculture, few people know

where it is. The mountain villages all command breathtaking views of the sea. We drove up the mountain and through the narrow streets of Lachi to eat dinner at Matoula's Taverna. Sitting under the arbor that supports a massive grapevine, just above the main church in the center of town, we listened to the melodies of Manos Hatzithakis and Yianni Spanos, while savoring Matoula's delectable Greek dishes: feta cheese wrapped in eggplant, *tsaiti* (cheese and spinach pie), *tsatziki* (yogurt, cucumber & garlic dip) and freshly-caught fried *kalamari* (squid).

Lachi was originally a Byzantine village built in the shadow of Mt. Vavila, close to a spring called Avlos, which supplied water to several nearby settlements. The Byzantine chapel of Aghios Georgios of Vavila contains frescoes of scenes from the Old and New Testaments. Like many of the surrounding villages, the inhabitants are mainly fishermen and farmers cultivating olives. Masses of magenta bougainvilleas provide a striking contrast to the whitewashed walls of the houses along its narrow streets.

Journal Entry: Sunday, July 2
While the church bells of Aghia Triada tolled at eight this morning, the town of Neapoli continued to sleep soundly after a festive Saturday night. Even the cicadas were quiet for a change. After breakfast, we drove to Pounta beach, opposite the island of Elafonisos, for a long midday swim in turquoise waters. We enjoyed a leisurely stroll along the soft white sandy beaches next to the now-submerged prehistoric chamber tombs. There were few

bathers on the beach today. Not even the Caretta-caretta turtle, a frequent visitor to these sandy beaches, was in sight.

Pounta beach is about a kilometer and a half to the southeast of the village of Aghios Georgios, opposite the island of Elafonisos and next to Strongili Limni (the Round Lake). The sand dunes and flora around the lake serve as natural barriers to the wind and wave action corroding the coast. Reeds, bamboo, and rare sea cedars grow alongside three plant species found only in this area, the *Goulimis* tulip, *Lenaria hellenica*, and *Linum leucanthemum* thyme, a species with purple and red leaves. Eighty species of birds have been spotted here; seventeen species nest around Lake Strongili.

Visible in the shallow waters offshore is the section of Vion submerged following a Bronze Age earthquake. There are chamber tombs two to three meters below the surface, opposite the islet Pavlopetri. In 1968, a Cambridge Underwater Exploration Group led by R.C. Jones discovered a small arched Roman bridge crossing the channel between Pounta beach and the island of Elafonisos. The bridge suggests the existence of a road of importance in ancient times, which probably went along the edge of the bay to what is now the island of Elafonisos.

Journal Entry: Monday, July 3

Today, Virginia opened the rustic wooden doors of her mountain home in Mesochori to a dozen writers. Under a Corinthian blue sky, the Greek Muses also welcomed their creative guests. The Muses smiled and caressed the spirit of each writer as she settled into the magic of this mountain retreat. Breathing in the intoxicating scents of oregano, marjoram, rosemary, and thyme, the writers were awed and inspired by the beauty of the spectacular Lakonian coastline. The wind was strong this afternoon. But no matter. The writers were ready to experience Greece, to find their stories in her story, to embark on their personal odysseys.

At the time of the census taken by the Venetian Francesco Grimani in the sixteenth century, Mesochori was the second most-populated settlement in Vatika. Then, as today, the primary sources of income were agriculture and livestock. During the Ottoman occupation, its economy remained strong. But as in other mountain settlements throughout Vatika, crumbling buildings now border Mesochori's narrow pathways. Homes were abandoned long ago, when inhabitants fled to larger settlements that offered better services, such as schools and clinics, and more prosperous economies. But today, the breathtaking view and peaceful atmosphere are drawing descendents back to this mountain settlement. Old homes are being reconstructed and refurbished. New homes are being built.

The tiny chapel of Aghios Theodoros dates back to the Byzantine period. It contains remnants of richly painted frescoes. Post-Byzantine churches include the Church of Transfiguration, the Church of Ipapanti, Aghia Paraskevi, and the small chapel at the base of the medieval castle, Aghios Spyridon. The historian A. Kastoris, in his 1939 book entitled, *I Epidayros Limira*, states that the castle was known as the "White Fortress" and was built by the Venetians, sometime after 1479.

Journal Entry: Tuesday, July 4

Tonight we visited the mountain village of Faraklo, two kilometers above Mesochori. We ate at El Faraklo, an outdoor taverna built of heavy oak beams and large granite stones. The owner, Panayiotis Billinis, serves his own versions of Greek *mezes* (tidbits), while diners sip local wine and listen to Greek melodies. Silhouetted against the late evening sky were the islands of Kythira and Elafonisos. Thousands of tiny lights glimmered in Mesochori, Neapoli and other scattered settlements. Faraklo is called the "Balcony of Vatika" and reminded us of Mt. Olympus, where the Gods reputedly stood. In the *Odyssey*, Homer wrote,

> *"Olympos, where the abode of the gods stands firm,*
> *and unmoving*
> *forever, they say, and is not shaken with winds, not*
> *spattered*
> *with rains, nor does snow pile ever there, but the*
> *shining bright air*
> *stretches cloudless away, and the white light*
> *glances upon it."*

Faraklo dates from the Middle Ages and, in the sixteenth century, was one of the largest towns in the Peloponnese. During the Ottoman occupation it was the most important settlement in the area, the seat of the Ottoman sultan and local Greek administrators. After liberation from the Ottoman Empire in 1821, Faraklo became the capital of the Municipality of Maleas, one of two municipalities in the region.

Today, many fine old stone buildings remain which bear witness to its historical importance. Ruins of Venetian buildings and even a mosque can still be found. The Byzantine churches of Aghios Stratis, Aghios Sarapis, and the smaller Aghios Nikolaos still stand, and some of them contain traces of Byzantine frescoes.

The spring in the middle of Faraklo continues to provide water for those who are willing to come and fill their water jugs. Vatika has many springs, and the water from each spring has a different flavor. The water from the Faraklo spring tastes slightly sweet.

Journal Entry, July 5

In the early morning, several writers set out to explore the hiking trails of Vatika. From Mesochori they trekked to Faraklo. After an hour searching for the continuation of the footpath to Paradisi, they gave up. The trail had disappeared—overgrown with weeds or blocked by a private landowner. So they walked along a dirt road that contoured around the hillside until they intersected another footpath to Paradisi. From there they walked down to Neapoli.

Everyone reconvened for the evening workshop. Later, we introduced the writers to a popular *ouzeria* on the boardwalk in Neapoli. Sipping ouzo cooled with ice and diluted with water, we nibbled grilled octopus and mussels, accompanied by tomato and cucumber salad and toasted French bread. And, of course, black, salty kalamata olives. We watched the moon rise over the wine-dark sea.

If you are not trekking the various footpaths to Paradisi, you can easily drive there on a newly paved road. The Church of the

Assumption dominates the main square. During the first two weeks of August, pilgrims come and stay in monastic cells to celebrate the feast of the Virgin Mary. Spring water cascades from the living rock, offering cool refreshment to visitors. People from throughout Vatika come regularly to fill up their jugs with the water, which is reputed to have healing qualities.

Journal Entry, July 6

In Book Three of Homer's *Odyssey*, Telemachus tells of his rough voyage with Menelaus from Cape Sounio to Cape Maleas. To this day, the seas of Cape Maleas can present a serious challenge to all sea-faring voyagers. Homer wrote,

> " . . . when he too had got away over the wine-dark sea in those great ships of his and had run as far as the steep bluff of Malea, Zeus, who is always on the watch, took it into his head to give them a rough time, and sent them a howling gale with giant waves as massive and as high as mountains."

Zeus watched over us, too, in a gentler frame of mind. It was a windy day when we left Neapoli. Captain Vassilis met us at the dock at ten in the morning. Holding on to our sun hats, swinging camera cases and beach bags, we boarded his large wooden *caique*, the *Vassilis Papoulis*, and motored to the island of Elafonisos for the day. We suffered neither giant waves nor howling gales, but the sea was definitely choppy as we crossed the white-capped Malean waters.

Many Greek islands lay claim to Homeric Sirens, Centaurs, and Cyclops. Tradition holds that Cyclops once inhabited the island of

Elafonisos. These one-eyed giants were notorious for harassing sailors who braved the waters of Cape Maleas. I thought about the Cyclops and what they really represent. The Greek poet Cavafy reminded me that I need not fear the presence of the Cyclops itself, but only the Cyclops within me: *"You will never meet unless you drag them with you in your soul, unless your soul raises them up before you."*

The island of Elafonisos is Vatika extending into the sea. It was once joined to the mainland by a narrow strip of land. The ancient travel writer, Pausanias, referred to it as *"a cape projecting out to sea thirty miles from Asopos called the Donkey's Jaw. There is a Sanctuary of Athene on it with no statue and no roof, supposed to have been built by Agamemnon, and Kinados' memorial: he was Menelaus's steersman."*

Though Pausanias called the island-promontory a donkey's jaw, it was later compared to an *"elafi,"* head of a deer. Hence the current name, Elafonisos. Its inhabitants have always been fishermen, seamen, and olive growers. Today it is a holiday resort. Its picturesque harbor is lined with fish restaurants and cafes. The two main tourist attractions of the island are its famous fish soup, *kakavia,* and its beautiful long sandy beaches: Simos to the south, Lefki to the east, and Tis Panaghias ta Nisia (the Virgin Islands) to the west. All the beaches are accessible by road. In the summer months, daily boat service to the beaches operates from the town of Elafonisos.

Journal Entry, July 7
Monemvasia has been said to reveal the face and soul of Greece. This medieval fortress is located on a rocky island off the east

coast of the Peloponnese, just fifty minutes by road northeast of Neapoli, at the edge of the Municipality of Vatika. Also called the "Gibraltar of the East," it is often compared with its rocky cousins, Mont St. Michel in France and St. Michael's Mount in England. One can sense the history embedded between the ancient stones of the fading burnt sienna walls of Monemvasia.

Sitting at a café on one of the narrow cobble-stoned streets, I looked straight up towards Aghia Sophia at the top of the rugged cliff. I had to cover my eyes from the glare of the afternoon sun reflected off the Sea of Myrtoo. I reflected on these lines written by Monemvasia's native son, Yiannis Ritsos, in his celebrated poem, *Romiosini,*

> *"These trees cannot adjust to lesser sky,*
> *these storms cannot adjust beneath the tread of strangers,*
> *these faces cannot adjust unless they feel the sun,*
> *these hearts cannot adjust unless they live in justice."*

Monemvasia was founded in the sixth century by people seeking refuge from the Slavic and Arabic invasion of Greece. Until the fifteenth century, it flourished as a leading commercial port and fortress under the Byzantine Empire. After that, like the rest of Vatika, the Venetians and Ottomans ruled over it in intervals.

The name Monemvasia derives from two Greek words, *monem* and *emvasia,* meaning "single entrance." That is how one enters this huge rocky mound, an island pounded by the surrounding sea. Passing through the narrow archway protected by two heavy iron-plated wooden gates dating back to the sixteenth century, the visitor walks along narrow cobble-stoned streets and ducks under vaulted archways. Old Venetian chimney pots and terracotta-tiled rooftops are silhouetted against the sky. Luggage is carried by donkey through the pedestrians-only town. A single cannon, an ancient church, and a new museum surround the center square.

Houses with Venetian and Ottoman architectural features have been faithfully reconstructed, and it is not uncommon for Byzantine elements to be preserved in the basement. The houses are two- or three-storied with basements and tiled roofs. At the lowest level, which is always vaulted, is the cistern for collecting rainwater and the storage cellar. The ground floor houses the living room and kitchen. The upper story is usually one large room separated into bedrooms by reed and plaster partitions or hanging curtains.

Journal Entry, July 8

A jeep and two taxis drove us through the winding mountain roads of Vatika. Our first stop was the neolithic cave of Kastania. In the early 1900's, a shepherd in search of water discovered the cave. The writers, like the shepherd, were awe-inspired by the color and magnificence of thousands of cone-shaped stalactites hanging over their heads and the stalagmites, like heads of mushrooms, crowding the undulating floor of the cave.

Later we drove over the mountain ridge of Ano and Kato Kastania to the small fishing hamlet of Aghios Ilias. Along the coastline of Aghia Marina lies the Petrified Forest. Expecting to see a miniature Sherwood in stone, we finally discovered several trunks of petrified trees on a rock cliff overhanging the cove of Aghia Marina.

That evening the writers learned how to Greek dance on a limestone balcony in Neapoli. The *kalamatiano* is performed in a circle and originated in the Peloponnesian district of Kalamata. It is an ancient mainland dance cited in inscriptions at Delphi from the first century A.D. Bravura turns and sidelong leaps are performed by the leader, while the dancers follow in smooth rhythmic steps. The *hassaposervikos* was originally a butcher's dance in Constantinople during the Byzantine era. As in the *hora,* kicks alternate with cross-steps to a fast and often strenuous tempo.

Ano Kastania (upper Kastania) is a picturesque village situated at the top of a large gorge leading down to a pleasant beach. The existing village replaced the original settlement, which was destroyed by pirates in the Byzantine era. Traces of Byzantine frescoes are still evident in the church of Aghios Panteleimon. The village of Kato Kastania (lower Kastania) hovers on the hillside below Ano Kastania. Both villages derive their income from the surrounding farmland and grazing of livestock; tiers of olive groves and citrus trees extend across the mountain slopes.

The road passing Kato Kastania leads to the cave of Kastania. Guided tours are scheduled daily during summer months and on Saturdays only during the rest of the year. Visitors delight in the nooks, the ceilings and the parlors, the incredible forms and fantastic shapes of the stalactites and stalagmites dating back over three million years.

The Petrified Forest—a collection of tree trunks millions of years old—is located near Aghia Marina, where Cape Maleas projects into the sea. The ground in which they stand is made up of a vast number of fossilized shells, which create a kind of natural mosaic.

Journal Entry, July 9

Thanasis drove through the eye of Daemonia to find his Muses in paradise. He talked of myth, poetry, the Greek god Dionysus, and Bacchaen rituals. It was time to dance. Though Dionysus was impetuous, unreflective and, at times, irrational, he was passionate. He expressed his passions through music and dance. Our spirits were undoubtedly aligned with that of Dionysus as we celebrated the night at the taverna Neraida in Aghios Nikolaos.

An important characteristic of Greek dance is its intimate relationship between words and music. This relationship governed the movements of the dancing chorus of the ancient Greek tragedies. At the Neraida, a young bouzouki player and a guitarist played lively Greek tunes and we opened our souls to the passions of the dance. Plato wrote,

"The dance, of all the arts, is the one that most influences the soul. Dancing is divine in its nature and is the gift of the gods."

The village of Aghios Nikolaos is in the center of a fertile farming region known for its Byzantine monasteries and ruined chapels. It has often been called a small Mt. Athos. The frescoes and decorated dome of the tiny chapel of Aghios Georgios, built right into the cliff face above Cape Maleas, are still in good condition. A few meters away is the monastery of Aghia Irini, perched on a terrace overlooking the sea. Other Byzantine chapels in the region are Aghios Ioannis, the Evangelistria, and Aghios Efstathios. Post-Byzantine chapels include Aghios Georgios Katzileris, Aghia Marina, and Aghios Dimitris.

Journal Entry, July 10

This evening the writers were invited to sample wines produced in the region of Vatika from Greek varieties of grapes. We learned how to describe the color, appearance, nose, and taste of eight different red and white wines. At dinner, we raised our glasses in appreciation with a toast to fine Greek wines. We were reminded of the Five Senses of the Cup:

Sight: The color of the wine
Smell: The wine
Taste: The wine
Touch: The cup
Sound: The clinking of glasses

Journal Entry, July 11

In Mesochori, under a luminescent full moon, Virginia danced her *zeibekiko,* the quintessential solo dance of the free spirit. Like Selene (the moon) in her heavenly chariot, Virginia glowed with energy and light. Reluctant to leave, the writers felt like Boss in Kazanzakis's *Zorba the Greek.* They were returning home, but they had learned to dance, experienced passion, embraced and accepted life. Venturing through Vatika, each writer had experienced her own odyssey.

A Kiss

C.K. McFerrin

I was nervous as we waited for a woman named Virginia. We were staying in her home for ten days. She wasn't home, and no one knew the way to her house. On top of a mountain, at the dead-end of a road wide enough for only one car, sat our fourteen-seat bus. A round mulberry tree, strategically placed, separated it from a steep, ridged walking path within the village of Mesochori.

I had heard only a little about Virginia from Connie, our Greek host and writing workshop organizer: "She is very special. You'll love her home. Wait until she sings. She dances the tango. She has magic."

She sounded mythical, and I began to paint my own picture of this sophisticated Greek woman—successful, beautiful, elegant, and enchanting. She lived on the mountain and accumulated power from the land, the winds, and the Aegean Sea. The more I thought about her, the more intimidated I felt, wondering how I would be able to communicate with this goddess.

Jet-lagged and confined for five hours on a bus ride from Athens to Mesochori, along the two-lane highway, by way of the coastal town Neapoli, left me, and the writing group I was traveling with, very weary. Only a thin veil separated us from our emotions and our reactions to unexpected events. Everyone was edgy with anticipation. In the hot afternoon sun, grateful to be out of the bus, I walked around the perimeter of this sudden end point.

On one side of the road was a ledge guarded by a thick steel rail, painted bright yellow—hopefully bright enough to prevent the unsuspecting traveler from the steep drop. Opposite the lookout was the tall retaining wall of a neighbor's backyard, privileged and graced with hillside views of olive trees in military green, shimmering in the Greek sunlight. Dry scrub brush and grasses, strokes of golds and browns, dappled with colored blossoms of yellows, purples and blues, blended together on a canvas of red clay and lichen-covered stone. I could smell a dry sweetness from the hot summer day.

Red, black, green, large, small, wheeled, or carry-on—our cases were strewn around in disarray like a bulky game of pick-up sticks. Cell phone calls were being made by Barbara, our leader and the other organizer of the workshop, to locate Virginia. Barbara's voice and manner were calm and even-toned in contrast to the looks people started giving each other and the few barbed comments that began to creep out as the time passed. I just walked.

"No, she's not here, have you talked to her?" she asked Connie. Her expression let us know it was still a mystery. So we waited, with anticipation and curiosity rising like the heat from the road.

'How could someone who was expecting a group of women for ten days not be home?' I thought. 'Even when I'm having a few people over for a little dinner I'm frantic to make sure I'm ready. And my preparation usually takes me up to the last minutes before their arrival. I cannot imagine not being here for a group like us. Is that what makes you a goddess? You have it all together. You can go for a swim.' I, like the others, was tired and hot and a bit cranky, wondering what was in store.

"Is that her?" someone from the group blurted out. We all turned our heads and raised our hands to our eyes to block the sun. We looked like we were saluting. Way off in the distance, a small car was seen buzzing around a corner. The only car on the road heading up the hill, it had to be her.

"Was that a little Toyota?" I mumbled to myself, "Yes; silver; four-door."

We could see her every switchback turn as she climbed the mountain. There was hardly any traffic in this country region, so any car up the road was an announcement. I learned later that local people built their villages on the hillsides for just this reason, so they could spy the approach of threatening pirates coming into Neapolis Bay.

My gaze followed along the road that crisscrossed down the mountain, to the low whitewashed buildings of Neapoli, a town shaped loosely like a triangle. Its base follows along the sparkling blue coastline. Its northern and southern points look as if they can no longer be contained and ooze out beyond their original structure. Boats in Neapolis Bay sit in a holding pattern, I later learned, sheltered from the *meltemi*, the strong and sometimes violent winds that blow through this region and remind us that the gods still rule the land. Beyond the bay are the islands, Elafonisos and Kythira, both rich in natural beauty and mythic lore.

As I continued to walk the perimeter of our landing, I could hear the motor of a car racing at what sounded like a very high speed. Finally, and all of a sudden, I turned my head, and the silver bullet of a car crested the road and almost killed me, coming to a screeching stop at my feet! Like one of the local grasshoppers, I jumped out of the way just in the nick of time. The Goddess had arrived!

The car door opened and out exploded Virginia. She was petite with even-toned bronze skin, I imagined creamy to the touch. Her hair was cut to the base of her neck, an uptown style. She looked like she had just come up from the beach in a snow-white strapless, terry cover-up that allowed us to see her white bikini bathing suit underneath. She was a bolt of lightning and energy to this weary group and everyone paused briefly.

Bursting into a greeting, she first kissed our driver, George, on both cheeks. He towered over her as she wrapped her sculpted arms around him in a warm embrace, punctuated by their Greek exclamations.

I have always loved the way people from other countries greet each other, taking time for the warm gentle kiss, first on one cheek, then the other. How was it that America, with the influx of so many Europeans, had lost this manner of greeting, this intimate way of welcoming one another into heart and home?

Then, Virginia turned to look at the group spread out over the area. She stopped and slowly took us in, as if she had cast a net into the sea. Capturing us, she pulled us together with the warmth of her eyes, each one into her world of Greece, of Mesochori. Turning, she began at the far end of the group. I watched. She introduced herself first with a smile as wide as Neapoli below. Then she reached out to gently shake hands. Leaning in, she gave a kiss to each cheek, a "welcome blessing," dabbing a little of herself like a perfume behind the ears. Each person smiled and looked as if they had known her forever, their movements smooth and confident. I began to fidget as she made her way, one by one, up the line, gazing into each person's eyes like one does at the end of a church service, thanking the priest for his insights and blessings.

I was last. I don't know how that happened. Now my turn, I suddenly was very aware of the heat of the afternoon, feeling weary, and a bit overwhelmed by the loud and constant singing of the cicadas all around. Virginia greeted me. Her smile was a welcome framed by her tanned narrow face. Her brown eyes were the color of the landscape and as broad and encompassing, if that is even possible. She was shorter than I was, petite, graceful in her casual white. Our hands met first. Her handshake was delicate. I leaned in to my right to meet her cheek. As I did, she leaned to her left. We were headed toward a kissing collision! I got flustered. I countered my slight mix up by going to the opposite side. She, too, adjusted to her opposite and we were headed for a second collision, when I bumped her nose with mine. The third correction fell short and I planted a big smooch right on her lips. I pulled back, shocked and embarrassed, heat rising to my already red face. Her brown eyes widened briefly in surprise.

George the driver belted out a loud hoot that could be heard along each turn of the switchbacks down the hill. He spoke in Greek and his hands were shaking fiercely making fun of me. I knew it. My companions all broke into laughter. I, too, laughed out loud. I looked over at Alexa, the only Greek-American amongst us. She had known these ways for all of her eighteen years and she was cracking up. A major American *faux pas!* Virginia smiled a smile of the ocean. She took my shoulders square in her hands and looked me right in the eyes.

"No matter!" she said emphatically. She smiled again, big and broad. Her eyes sparkled, wiping my embarrassment away. Her power was in her kind and gentle way, and I realized, at that moment, that the spirit of Greece could be found in the openness and grace of a kiss.

A Village Cemetery

CATHERINE PYKE

❧

A small cemetery lies at the curve of a road beyond a church in the village of Mesochori. Wandering past the bell tower of the church, I came upon a maroon-colored wrought-iron gate enclosing twenty-seven raised marble graves arranged before a small chapel overlooking Neapolis Bay. Each grave looked like a stately bed with a headboard, topped by a marble cross. The headboard held a glassed-in cabinet, containing objects reflecting the person's life. Encased were religious icons, vases filled with flowers, an incense urn, and a delicately-framed photograph depicting the person in his or her prime. Symbols for those who made their living by the sea, a small boat, an anchor, the captain's wheel of a ship, adorned the marble tombs of fishermen and sailors.

I stood outside the gate, watching a middle-aged couple tend to the grave of their family. Something kept me from entering the cemetery. I'm not sure what it was. Could it be I hold on to the childish fear that the dead have the power to pull me down with them? It's impossible to escape the reminders, the roadside shrines to those lost along the narrow roads near cliffs above the sea, the clusters of graves on hillsides between villages. The signs are everywhere, though I'd rather not be reminded that the borderline from life to death is too easily and quickly crossed.

I watched the man swinging an urn of burning incense and sprinkling water over his family's tombstone. A fragrant smell permeated my senses, as he looked up and caught my eye.

"*Kalimera*," I said, in my gentlest voice, hoping he'd see I meant his family no disrespect. Wearing a tee-shirt, khakis and running shoes, my camera in hand, I was clearly a tourist. He nodded, muttered something I couldn't understand, and resumed swinging the incense urn. Drops of mist cooled my skin. The inebriating fragrance took me to another place and time.

A memory of my father enters my mind. I see him leaning against his parents' headstone, a look of indescribable sadness on his face. We'd taken fresh flowers, peonies from our garden, to my grandparents' graves. Looking past the cemetery now, into the shimmering sea, I remember how my father loved Greece. Through long Utah winters, he and my mother read piles of books on the history and archeological treasures of Greece and conversed over cocktails about Lord Byron's adventures in Corfu. Around this time, my father learned to fly a small plane and dreamed of escaping a life too colorless for a man nearing forty. He wanted me to fly, too, gave me flying lessons for my fourteenth birthday. I've lived more than three times the age of that fourteen-year-old now, yet a part of me still yearns, like my father, to feel myself fully alive.

I took only one flying lesson, on the day before the commercial plane that was to bring my father home collided with another in fire above the San Gabriel mountains, killing everyone on board. In one moment defying statistical probability, I lost my father, the one who dared me to live. Following his death, I lived my life cautiously.

Leaving the cemetery, I walked back to our writer's workshop, near the top of a mountain alive with sounds and color—screeching cicadas, vistas of olive groves, a constant, low roaring wind that lifts chairs and an occasional goat from one terrace level to another. I entered the whitewashed home that is anchored against the mountainside like a cliff dwelling. Virginia, our host, greeted me and asked me about my walk. I told her about the cemetery.

"It's lovely," I said, "peaceful. But I don't know any of the villagers. I feel no right to be there."

"You can go there," she insisted. Her face lit up as if she'd discovered a secret that could save the world, but that she's generous enough to squander on the one person who needed it most. She turned, reached above her refrigerator, pulled down three heavy pots. The largest was a cauldron of pounded copper and two shallower ones used for making cheese and spinach pies.

"*Bakiria*," she said, using their Greek name.

Next she showed me a fired clay vessel, *pythori*, used to store olives and cheeses.

"I love them," she said, exuding joy. She began to tell me their story.

One day, Virginia was driving along in her favorite car, a two-cylinder Citroen, when she came upon a pile of abandoned furnishings. The rubbish had been left near a house whose previous owner, an elderly woman, had recently died. The new owners, desiring their own furnishings, had thrown out the entire contents of the woman's home. Each piece in the pile called out to Virginia. In addition to pots, she found a table and twelve carpets. She struggled with the pieces and managed to fit them into her car. She took two carpets at a time to the sea and placed them in the water. Immersed in salt water for many hours and dried in the sun, the vivid colors in the carpets came back to life.

"She was a happy person," Virginia said of the woman for whose belongings she had found places in her own home.

"I found her radio. She loved music."

And yet, Virginia knew that the woman had experienced a sad life. She had found the woman's identity card in the pile and learned a little about her life from a friend of her mother's.

"What was the name on the card?" her mother's friend asked.

"Meimethi," Virginia responded.

"I knew her," came the reply. "She was always happy."

The woman whose possessions now graced Virginia's home was named Etamatika (Stamatiki, in shortened form) Meimethi. She had died at age ninety-four, leaving no descendents.

"She had no one to respect her things," Virginia said. By rescuing them from destruction, she was keeping the elderly woman's spirit alive.

"When we die, the spirit goes everywhere into the air." She explained that when the things we loved are protected, the spirit remains. "I'm happy to protect her things. I feel blessed to have them in my house."

The following day, Virginia walked with me to the cemetery. As we entered through the gate, she crossed herself and began to look for the marble tombstone. We looked carefully at every monument, large and small. The smaller stones, she explained, held the bones of those who had died many years ago. These are eventually removed to make room for the newly-dead. At last we came to the monument that held the remains of the happy woman.

"Here she is," Virginia said. The photograph in the glass cabinet showed a woman of about fifty, over forty years prior to her death. She had a slim face and thin lips that seemed naturally to form a smile, defying the usual formality of portraits. The engravings in stone told part of her story. She was married to Dimitri, who died in 1957 at age sixty-three. His family name was Turkish. There is no record of her parents' name. Stamatiki lived alone as a widow for thirty-two years. Her two children, daughters Sophia and Elena, died within a year of each other—Elena, at age one in 1937, Sophia, age ten, the following year.

Stamatiki was born in 1895, shortly after Sparta became the capital of Lakonia, during the reign of King Otto I, and died in 1989, the year the wall fell in Berlin. Her lifetime spanned occupations by Venetians, Ottomans, Germans, and the return of independence to Greece. Most likely, she lived through severe earthquakes and endured periods of near-starvation. But the stones remain silent, the essential details of her life, indiscernible. Who her parents were and the village she came from remain mysteries, as does the reason, perhaps a disease like malaria or typhoid, that her little girls were taken away from her.

On the day the taxi drove us back to Athens, I took one last walk to the cemetery. Fresh flowers in hand, I swung open the gate and entered to fill the empty urns on the Meimethi monument. During the long journey home, Stamatiki's smile lingered in my mind. I hoped a little part of her would stay with me: the choices of joy over sadness, life over death, and the courage to throw caution to the winds and feel myself fully alive.

A California Gardener Goes to Greece

ANNE WOODS

Ɔ⌐

I came to Greece to find paradise. I came to rub between my fingers the scents of this place: wild thyme, oregano, rosemary, allium, and mint, and to inhale their life.

The garden is a sanctuary for me. Where there are no plants I feel an emptiness, a lack of connection with the earth. Gardens bring me joy. Watching plants germinate and grow, and nurturing them, is my peace. They are also a connection to family. The delicate smell of iris recalls my maternal grandmother; the full and heavy scent of red roses, my paternal grandmother. These smells take me back to childhood.

My own gardening began when I could first hold a trowel. A

small plot of dirt in my mother's vegetable garden, between the comfrey and tomatoes, became my own. Here I planted my first flowers: zinnias, gladioli, and four o'clocks.

"There is more to this than just growing flowers," my grandmother said while helping me plant one afternoon. "You'll understand when you're older." What, I wondered, could be more exciting than watching a flower bud open into a bloom? Gardening was a purely hedonistic endeavor for me then.

In my garden now, in northern California, I have these same flowers. There are also the greens and yellows and reds of vegetables. It is more than a mix of heady scents and tasty vegetables; it makes me feel alive. But, it is my childhood garden that I remember as paradise. Life seemed at once as profound and as simple as the fragrance of basil crushed between my fingers and mixed with the clean odor of tomato leaves. It is still my favorite smell, after thirty-one years of rubbing leaves and sniffing plants and flowers like a seamstress checking the quality of a bolt of silk.

I have planted many gardens, always striving to create the feel of those first ones, and never achieving the exact proportions, like a baker who has lost her recipe. The landscape of the Mediterranean has always beckoned me, as though examining it first hand would unlock the meaning of my grandmother's admonishment.

As my flight descended over the Aegean Sea, on approach to Athens, I caught my first glimpse of the geography of Greece. The land looked bleached, the color of ivory, from my perch ten thousand feet above it. The Aegean was a brilliant blue, as though it was a pool of watery sapphires. As we descended lower, the ivory and sapphires met with the first traces of green. The scrubby vegetation was grey-green. It was the subdued green of plants that have evolved to survive in heat and dryness.

After eight or nine millennia of habitation, agriculture, and overgrazing by sheep and goats, the landscape of Greece has changed. In many areas, particularly the coastal plains and hills, forests have given way to a maquis landscape of evergreen shrubs. Oleanders, junipers, evergreen oak, bay, and olive are common, especially in the southern part of the country. Closer to the ground, mounds of thyme, covered in pale purple flowers during summer, grow among other wild herbs such as sage and oregano.

I looked down on the landscape filled with the excitement that comes with discovering a place for the first time. Athens lies 38 degrees north of the equator, the same latitude that runs through my home in Marin County, just north of San Francisco. I searched for similarities, but saw few here, southeast of Athens. From above, my first glimpses of Greece reminded me of the desert landscape of Mexico's Baja peninsula. Much more lushness was waiting for me than I had first spotted through the window of the Lufthansa Airbus.

But when I arrived in Athens, I was disappointed. The July heat was so oppressive that I imagined the earth baking as though it was one giant pancake. The hills were arid and rocky. Their beige color melted into the hazy sky at midday. Modern, high rise apartment buildings, a slightly lighter shade of beige, thrust headlong into the sky. The sprawling city appeared as if it had been washed out by the sun, cooked over and over, like a twice-baked potato, its monuments preserved by dry heat. Could I find paradise here I wondered?

Two days later we, a group of women writers embarking on a ten-day workshop, left Athens by bus and drove to the southeastern most point of the Peloponnese, the region called Vatika. Once outside the city, I began spotting magenta and white oleanders, and wild anise. Queen Anne's lace was at the height of its bloom cycle. The lacy white flowers hovered above thick stalks like ladies' parasols. Wild thistle, seed heads waving in the wind like desiccated artichokes, lined the fields along the road. Olive and fig trees appeared. These plants are familiar to me, many also growing in my native northern California. Even among the dry, wild grasses I recognized two species which grow in California. Though they have gone wild in California, they are not indigenous. In southern Greece, 36 degrees 30' north of the equator, I found a countryside so comforting in its familiar smells and flora that I felt immediately at ease, even though I was half a globe away from home.

When we arrived at our destination, the mountainous village of Mesochori, I was awestruck. The late afternoon sun shone through the sieve of a cloud, spreading out into rays that descended to Neapolis Bay several miles away. It looked as if Zeus's Mt. Olympus was hovering behind the cloud.

Mesochori is about one thousand feet up the western face of a mountain, overlooking the seaside town of Neapoli. By car, fifteen minutes of switchbacks lie between the two. From the air, the Cape Maleas peninsula looks like a plump finger, reaching out into the confluence of the Ionian Sea to the west and the Aegean Sea to the east. "Round Malea and forget your country," goes an ancient Greek saying. It was the fiercely shifting winds of Cape Maleas that blew Odysseus off course.

A small collection of houses, white stucco with red tile roofs, cling to the rocky cliffs in Mesochori. There is a small church, though it was closed much of the time I was there. A grocery store, post office, and loud noises are absent. The gardens are sprawling and unbound, melding seamlessly with the natural landscape of Vatika. I was bewitched by this harmony.

It was morning in Mesochori. A gusty summer *meltemi* wind was whipping up the mountainside, carrying with it the clean and pungent smell of wild herbs. I tied my hair back with a scarf and began walking down the dirt road toward the small, white church called Aghia Sotira, at the edge of the village. I looked down the mountainside at haphazardly laid out groves of olive trees. Some were in rows and others were scattered about wherever there was a hospitable plot of land. Their long, pointy leaves shimmered in the wind like schools of sardines turning through the cerulean blue sky.

My body warmed in the sun. The *meltemi* whirled around me, brushing the excess heat off my bare arms. I imagined paradise as I stopped at a fig tree. Green, unripe figs and fat, emerald green leaves grew out of a squat trunk. I touched the firm body of a fig (*siko*). It was already warm from the morning sun. I imagined this warmth in my mouth, the first bite severing the raspy, aubergine colored skin, my mouth discovering the honey sweet inside. Seeds crunched between my teeth. I imagined I swallowed, wanting more. I ran my fingers over the green fig. I felt teased that it wouldn't be ripe for another month, not until August. Longingly, I searched the tree for a ripe, soft fig. I peered between the leaves, like a blue jay after red raspberries.

Wild allium (*Kremidia agria*) grew along the road. Their tall, succulent stalks were each covered with a single lavender purple pom pom. Queen Anne's lace grew among them. Wild blackberries covered a retaining wall in front of a small house. The blackberry flowers were pink, not white as they are in my garden. A rooster crowed from a shanty coup in the backyard. Rosemary, dill, and oregano grew alongside a wild rose with miniature pink blossoms. *Horta*, the Greek term for a wide range of edible greens, grew wild, even sprouting from between rocks. This particular specimen appeared to be a cross between spinach and buckwheat. Grapes covered arbors over patios, and cascaded down hillsides. Olive trees compete with fig trees for position. There were several evergreen oaks, shorter and more compact than the native California varieties. There was a quince tree, and also pomegranate (*rodi*) trees in yards. The *rodi* fruit was small and green, but when ripe will be earthy red. I looked into a family's vegetable garden. Tall tomato (*domata*) plants were staked in circular wire cages. Broad-leafed zucchini (*kolokithakya*) plants were dotted with deep yellow blossoms (*kolokithoanthi*). Sweet green bell peppers (*piperya*), climbing cucumbers (*anguri*), and *horta* grew large in the plentiful sun.

In the orange glow of sunsets, as we sat with our host, Virginia, on her patio, she would often mash a wad of greenery in her delicate hands, and then open them for us to smell. Her hands moved from person to person, offering a perfume that made you think both of roast lamb and aromatherapy. The mixture was usually from the herb garden in front of her house: basil, lavender, rosemary, thyme, and oregano. Often she would add pungent *luisa* (lemon verbena) to the concoction. Sometimes she would offer a shiny, green leaf of *luisa* as an addition to a cup of tea. It infused the hot beverage with a lemony flavor more powerful than a lemon itself, but was neither sour, nor acidic. Herbs encircled Virginia's home. The herb garden in the front, the *luisa* on the side, a pot of basil (*vasilikos*) on the patio, and another by the kitchen sink created an aromatic bouquet and tasty additions to meals.

Vatika is the intersection of green and brown, of green and blue, of the lush and the dry. There is harmony between land and sea, sky and light. The landscape is organic. The gardens are not contrived, manicured, or artificial. There are no brilliant green lawns where nature cannot support them. Chemical fertilizers and insecticides are not used in the home garden. There is a soft and almost imperceptible transition from the cultivated to the feral. It is this wildness to which I am drawn.

It was the organic flow that struck me first. It is a flow not only within the land, but between land and people. The locals, Connie, Virginia, they all spoke of the land with conviction. It is part of their culture. They haven't lost that crucial link with the earth.

"Greeks love their gardens," said Connie, our Greek workshop host. "We love light and sun," she added. "We love to watch things grow. Greenery next to the blue of the sea, an electric pink bougain-villea vine against a whitewashed wall," she said are most beautiful to her. It is the Greek's humanization, I realize, of the mountains, the sea, the land, and the gardens that makes this place special. It is not just a lot of pretty flowers and fruits.

Perhaps this is what my grandmother meant all those years ago. Gardening keeps us grounded, humble. A garden, like a well-written book, can completely absorb you. It draws you in. It is a reconnection with the primal life forces of birth, growth, death, and regeneration. It marks changes in the weather, the passing of the seasons. The garden is a place of spiritual replenishment. It reminds us, gently, that we are members of a much larger community than just humankind.

Mulberry trees (*moura*) shaded the road as I approached the church. Their ripe fruit had fallen on the road, been trod upon, and made a midnight purple splatter painting upon its chalky surface. A heavily be-fruited walnut tree leaned over the last curve before I reached the church. I pulled a cluster of green walnuts, the size of small apples, toward me and breathed in their honey-sweet fragrance. The smell took me back to childhood, to the walnut trees in the yard of my parents' friends, the Tedeschis. I closed my eyes and lingered.

These memories of Vatika will germinate in my heart and by my hands they will grow in my own garden. I crushed in my hands the sprigs of thyme and basil I collected on my walk. I inhaled their cleansing, astringent aroma. I had found paradise.

Vines of Vatika

BARBARA J. EUSER

༂

"The Greek god Dionysus gave the gift of wine to man. He showed mortals how to cultivate vineyards, then he taught them the art of turning grapes into wine. Dionysus is a god of transformation: transforming grapes into wine and ordinary humans into beings filled with god, that is en-*theos*-asm, enthusiasm," Thanasis Maskaleris explained. An expert on Dionysus and Apollo, he shared his insights with us on the hillside in Mesochori. As he spoke, I looked at the tapestry of vineyards and olive groves on the slopes rolling down to the bright blue sea.

The Greeks learned Dionysus' lessons early on and learned them well. Indigenous varieties of grapes were cultivated and harvested and turned into a dark, sweet wine. In ancient times, enterprising Greek colonists and the ubiquitous Phoenician traders spread the art of cultivating vineyards and producing wine to the west as far as the Atlantic coast.

By the 1100's, large quantities of wines were being exported from the Peloponnese. The sweet wine made in Vatika near the island fortress of Monemvasia has been called "one of the most visible and enduring medieval Greek wines." As it was exported, its name evolved and it became known throughout Europe as malvasia or malmsey.

When the Byzantine Empire fell to the Crusaders in 1204, the European Crusaders gained access to Greek vineyards. In a second wave of exportation, Crusaders took local vines home with them, transplanting them throughout the Mediterranean basin, in Italy, France, Spain and Portugal.

By the mid-1400's, malmsey had become a popular wine in England and reputedly the favorite libation of the Royal Duke of Clarence. In Shakespeare's *Richard II*, when the First Murderer stabs Clarence, he says: "Take that, and that: if all this will not do, I'll drown you in the malmsey-butt within." And rumor has it Clarence drowned.

When Spanish explorers reached the New World, they carried with them grape vines from the Mediterranean basin—some of them varieties that had originated in Greece. By the mid-1500's, Greek grape vines were growing in Mexico, Brazil, Argentina, Panama, Peru and Chile.

Back to the Roots

Grape vines still thrive in the climate of Vatika. In Greece, there are basically two types of climates in which vines thrive: inland climates such as in the highlands near Tripoli and island climates where the sea winds cool the sun-warmed hillsides. From a grapevine's point of view, Vatika, with its long shoreline, is an island climate.

In the Biblical book of Isaiah it says, "And every man beneath his vine and fig tree shall live in peace and unafraid." The grapevine and the fig tree are symbols of security and the good life that may be enjoyed in times of peace. In Vatika, grapevines and fig trees have traditionally surrounded every whitewashed house. Making wine following the grape harvest in September was a family tradition. There is a self-sufficiency in Vatika that, coming from the United States, I always associated with pioneers. Now I realize the pioneers were only carrying on the traditional ways they had learned from their own ancestors. In Vatika, that meant growing one's own grapevines for wine, one's own olive trees to produce olives for the table and for olive oil, one's own lemons for flavoring all foods, and fig trees for figs to be eaten fresh or dried.

The process of making wine can be described simply: one crushes the ripe grapes, puts them into a barrel with yeast, allows the yeast to ferment using the sugar from the grapes, and decants the fermented juice into bottles for consumption. But then one must consider all the variables that go into creating not just an alcoholic grape juice, but a clear, aromatic, flavorful wine. That is where winemaking becomes an art.

A household winemaker may cultivate a few rows of grapevines that produce only a few hundred kilos of grapes. But the ratio of finished wine to grapes is almost three-quarters to one. So a few hundred kilos of grapes will yield a few hundred kilos of wine. Or, since one kilo is the weight of one liter of wine, a few hundred liters of wine—sufficient to meet a family's annual needs.

At the household level of winemaking, the grapes may be crushed by hand, if few enough, or by foot, as seen in old movies. At the hardware store in Neapoli, one can buy a grape crushing machine. The grapes used to be fermented, aged and transported in barrels of oak, pine or chestnut. Then plastic barrels replaced wood for household use. A backyard shed may serve as the wine *cava*, where the barrels sit in dark, cool shade until the fermented wine is drawn off into glass bottles, or even recycled plastic ones, and refrigerated until consumed.

At the end of August, I was invited to a small farm just outside Neapoli for the grape pressing. Kyrio Psarakis (Mr. Psarakis) grows thirty different varieties of grapes in small plots scattered through his olive grove. All thirty go into his homemade wine. By the time I arrived at nine in the morning, the grapes had been cut and dumped into the *lino*, a square concrete vat with a brass spigot in one corner. A young man wearing rubber boots, Spiro, was walking on the grapes, squashing the juice out of them. Years ago, the *lino* would have been built of stone, but Kyrio Psarakis' concrete *lino* is large and flat-bottomed and easy to clean. When about two inches of juice had accumulated in the bottom of the *lino*, the spigot was opened and grape juice flowed into a plastic bucket. As soon as one bucket filled, Kyrio Psarakis' brother replaced it with another. Meanwhile, Kyrio Psarakis and his grandson, Nikolas, carried the full bucket of juice to his *cava*, a room built on the garden level underneath the house. With Nikolas steadying the screen-bottomed funnel, Kyrio Psarakis poured the juice into the smallest of his three plastic wine barrels.

"This one holds one hundred and twenty kilos," Kyrio Psarakis told me. Gesturing to the other corners of the cool room, he said, "That one holds two hundred and forty kilos and the big one, three hundred." That should be plenty of wine for one family, I thought.

He stirred the juice with his hand, keeping the skins from clogging the funnel. When all the juice had flowed into the barrel, he squeezed out the skins and dropped them into another plastic bucket. "For distilling *tsipouro*," he said. "It tastes even better than ouzo."

"How long does the juice take to turn into wine?" I asked.

"Sixty-five days total," he responded. "After it ferments for about thirty days, I put the lid on the barrel very tight and wait another thirty-five days. Then I open this spigot and pour a glass. I taste it. If I am lucky, it tastes very good."

But the wine-pressing did not end with a single trodding. Spiro had shoveled all the skins and twigs into one corner of the *lino*. He put down a bunch of straight branches that reminded me of a large whiskbroom. Then he shoveled some skins onto the branches and covered them with more branches. He stepped heavily on the branches and once more juice flowed out the drain into a plastic bucket. When the trickle slowed, he lifted up the branches and shook out the grape skins, depositing them in another corner of the *lino*. He worked his way down the pile.

While Spiro was finishing with that stage of juice extraction, Kyrio Psarakis was assembling his grape press. This looked like a circle of barrel staves with spaces in between. The staves sat on a large metal saucer with a spout in its lip. A tall screw rose out of the center of the press. Spiro shoveled the remains of the grape skins into the grape press. Kyrio Psarakis packed the skins down tightly with his hands. When about half of the large pile of skins had been stuffed into the press, the lid was fitted on. Then he carefully stacked six wooden blocks on top and began tightening the screw. Slowly, carefully, lest the wooden blocks slip out of position, Kyrio Psarakis and his brother worked the press. A new trickle of grape juice flowed out of the barrel staves into the metal saucer and down into a plastic barrel. When juice stopped flowing, the press was opened and more skins shoveled in.

Nothing was wasted. Every drop of juice made it into the fermenting barrel. The skins were saved to make *tsipouro*. Only sixty-four more days to go until Kyrio Psarakis and his family will be enjoying this year's vintage.

A Step Beyond

Yiannis Vatistas came from a fishing family in the Vatika town of Aghia Marina, close to the remote tip of land that juts out into the sea and is known as Cape Maleas. Like every other family, the

Vatistas grew grape vines. Yiannis took charge of producing the family wine. But unlike most family wine producers, Yiannis became fascinated working with the vines. He enlarged the family vineyard and experimented with producing more and higher quality wine. His wine became known as the best around. He soon produced enough to be sold at the fish restaurant his family owned in Athens. Then other restaurants began to offer his wine. The more time Yiannis spent in his vineyards, the more he wanted to learn. He began researching the varieties of grapes that had been grown traditionally in Vatika and expanded his plantings to include *Assyrtiko, Aghiorghitiko* and *Roditis.*

In 1996, he realized he could not do it all. He hired an experienced oenologist, one of the first Greek women oenologists, Mary Flerianou, as his winemaker. Trained as a chemist, Mary contributed not only her chemist's skills, but her aesthetic expertise in the art of winemaking.

By that time, Yiannis had over sixteen hectares of Greek and French varieties of grapes under cultivation. He was no longer producing only taverna-style barrel wine, but had moved into the realm of commercial bottled wines. He blended *Chardonnay* and *Cabernet Sauvignon* with local varieties of grapes to produce flavorful white and red table wines.

Mary joined Yiannis after working at other Greek wineries for twenty years. She had developed her own philosophy about the best potential for Greek wines. She pushed Yiannis to go back to his roots and refocus on the local Greek varieties, believing that that is where Greek wines can enjoy a competitive advantage in the world market place. And so Yiannis planted *Petroulianos, Kydonitsa, Athiri, Monemvasia, Malvazia, Malagouzia, Thrapsa,* and *Mavroudi* varieties.

As a team, Mary and Yiannis continued to expand the market for Vatistas wines. And Yiannis continued to expand his vineyards. Moving along the Vatika coast to the west, he planted ten hectares of vineyards below the town of Pandanassa, on hillsides just above the sea. He also established vineyards farther north along the peninsula, near Monemvasia.

With seven years of experience, Yiannis began to enter Vatistas wines in international competitions. The medals began to accumulate: bronze in Thessaloniki 2001; two silvers in Brussels 2001; silver in Thessaloniki 2004; gold and silver in Brussels 2004; silver in Thessaloniki 2005; Gran Menzione in Vinitaly 2006; and special recognition in Japan 2006.

Mary's vision proved correct. The wines winning the top international prizes were *Assyrtiko, Kydonitsa,* Vatistas *Cabernet/Aghiorghitiko, Petroulianos,* Red Regional wine of Monemvasia and Fume. The vines of Vatika are proving as resilient and vital as the now-restored fortress of Monemvasia.

While Yiannis Vatistas has become the major commercial winemaker in Vatika, nearly every extended family continues to proudly produce wine of its own. The spirit of Dionysus is alive. Wine is an intrinsic part of life in Vatika, whether one is a household winemaker, or simply someone who appreciates the final product.

"Dionysus' body was torn apart each winter," Thanasis concluded, "Then reborn each spring." Every year, grapevines sprout new shoots, leaves, flowers that become grapes. The grapes are duly harvested and transformed into wine. The wine that was a crucial part of Dionysian celebrations is enjoyed by inhabitants and modern-day voyagers alike.

Meltemi

GAIL STRICKLAND

꒚

In my younger days, I wanted to be Zorba. To dance barefoot in the hot sand, the Aegean sun beating down on my head, arms flung wide to embrace life. For almost forty years, I've had a love affair with everything Greek: translating Homer in college, two visits to Greece, Greek festivals at home. Retsina, ouzo and homemade *souzoukakia* became the thread woven through my days. I wrote a novel about the oracle of Delphi, hoping the writing would unravel my mystery of a life not fully sung. I felt like I had been on a collision course. Husbands had abandoned me (two to be precise) and friends had turned and left without me understanding why. There was always something about the Greek song of life that felt like an answer. I simmered sweet *rizogalo* on the stove for hours, danced around the house stomping and clapping to bouzouki and toumbeleki . . . but only when no one was watching.

One evening at Izzy's, a pub in northern California after a Left Coast Writer's Salon, Lowry—a local publisher critiquing my Greek manuscript, looked up from the page and his beer and suggested, "See those ladies over there? You need to go introduce yourself, and, by the way," he shouted as I walked over to the table where three women sat eating fries, drinking wine and gesturing wildly. "Ask them about their trip."

꙳ ꙳ ꙳

Two months later, we pull into Mesochori, a small mountain hamlet just above the newer fishing village of Neapoli, in the southernmost Peloponnese—eleven women writers in our air-conditioned bus with Yiorgos, "George" at the wheel. We pile out into the afternoon heat and try to get ourselves and all our baggage down the rough stone path. Barbara, one of our intrepid leaders, looks like a pack mule as she bravely loads herself down with half of my bags. Having torn my meniscus a short time before this trip, getting down the drive with my luggage seems almost impossible.

Finally making it to Virginia's patio by doing my own stiff rendition of a Charlie Chaplin saunter, I take a deep breath: wild thyme and a dusky smell of fig and olive perfume the air. Rain clouds gather on the rock crags just above us. Cicadas call a cacophonous rhythm, escalating as the clouds grow darker, the hot afternoon air thickens. Below us, stretching to a distant grey horizon, is the sea, Neapolis Bay, where Odysseus, *polutropon*, the man of "many turns" struggled with gods and nature. Kythira, Aphrodite's island, is only a short distance offshore. Crete, Zorba's island, is lost in the mist beyond the far horizon.

Virginia greets us each with a kiss on both cheeks. "I was very happy to welcome you here. I was really open with a big smile to give you whatever I can, whatever I feel—my heart, my soul, my place." She welcomes strangers into her home with a warmth we will all learn to seek like a fire on a winter night, or the light of the candles she places later inside her white stucco hearth: red, brown, purple, all colors and sizes, three long tapers placed with care in a copper pot filled with sand. She is a *kore*, a goddess in white. In Greece, widows wear black, black for loss and sorrow. Though Virginia is widowed, she always wears white. White for her celebration of life, and because she *likes* to wear white. She looks great in white. It makes me wonder if I've been wearing black all these years, maybe not my dress or skirt or jeans, but inside where it matters the most. I go upstairs before dinner and change into the white shirt I bought in the Plaka, just to remind me.

After dinner. After folk songs in Greek and French sung by Virginia. After we make our own attempt to sing "Goin' to the Chapel" and "Bring It on Home," Colleen and I ascend the narrow stairs to heaven, our whitewashed room with an embroidery of Greek dancers on the wall, a stone floor, open wood beams, and white lace curtains between us and the sea. The warm wind blows stronger, laden with rain. And it is hot!

The first thing we do is open the windows, which proves to be more difficult than we thought it would be. One shutter falls off into Colleen's hands, but she's quick; saves it from falling onto the red tile roof and the patio below. She pulls it to the side, then holds the window open with her red carry-on case. But just as we succeed in keeping the window open, a strong gust of wind blows through the window and sucks the door open with a bang. I get up and close it. It bangs open again. Several times we take turns pulling our travel-weary bodies out of bed to close the wood door, only to have it bang open once more. We find a round stone left beside the door and try to block it closed, but our night is punctuated by great gusts of wind and the banging of shutters, the crashing of the door against the stone, closing, sucked open as another strong blast of wind roars through. Aeolus was definitely mocking us. The next morning before we wander bleary-eyed downstairs, the obvious occurs to me:

"Colleen, if we use the stone to hold the door open so the wind can blow through, instead of trying to stop the wind, the door doesn't bang." I laugh at myself and the first of many lessons the gods are cooking up for me. We had tried to stop the hot summer winds, the legendary *meltemi*, which drives the cargo ships to shelter in Neapolis Bay for days, shuts down ferry passages, drove Odysseus into the arms of Circe—we tried to stop it with our stone.

I join Virginia on the patio. She's wearing a silk slip and her jean jacket and is talking on the cell phone in rapid-fire Greek to French to English, but always back to Greek. She straightens the chairs. Tucks her hair behind her ears. "The wind. It took the chair, oh my God!" There is no bite to her words, no blame. She rushes down the stairs. "I go down to see their toilet." Soon she reappears with the chair and tucks a pillow behind my back, as I sit on the stone bench. "I'm fifty-two," she answers someone's question, and slips down the stairs again. I wonder how she is always helping, always giving and yet never gives herself away. Broken toilets and ten women writers sleeping on her sofas and beds, eating breakfast and lunch (sumptuous Greek salads and cheese pies and eggplant in fresh tomato sauce), nothing fazes her life of tangos and torch songs.

That evening we pile into taxis and head up the mountain to a hamlet, neighbor to Mesochori, rooted in the rock crags towering above Virginia's home. Faraklo: once the heart of Vatika, once a town with power to govern, with a school to instruct the young. It is a village like many others, with plots of land for vegetables, hens for eggs, roosters to sear outside the taverna on a grill—now rusted and neglected. In the center of the village there is a stone cistern. Spring water flows into the basin and I bend to hear the water fall against the earth. It was here at the spring that the village women gathered to fill their amphora, to talk and hug, but now I hear only shadow whispers of the women's laughter. Frogs chant their chorus. The *meltemi* blows, urging me to turn away, but I am reluctant to turn my back on the ghosts of the women who gathered at the spring. I want to share their stories—of husbands gone to war, children born. I want to tell them my own, to ask them if they still worry about their children. Did a time come when the *meltemi* freed them? Or was it only death. I listen for their answer, but hear only a brittle memory of red clay jugs clattering against stone.

I hold back one last moment from the conversation of my new friends, from the chain of life we brought up the mountain, crammed four abreast in the back seat of the taxi, singing along with Yiannis and bouzouki. I'm reluctant to bring the noise of the city, its clutter, tires spitting gravel, the smell of gasoline and technology. Time has passed by Faraklo. Moonlight washes across the sea far below. A hawk calls from the crags, as I turn to face the *meltemi* with its smell of the sea.

The next morning, as I sit on the patio outside our room, the wind blows off the cliffs above Mesochori, limestone brushed with "rosy-fingered dawn" as Homer would describe them. It blows my papers, tugs my hair into my eyes, but it brings me only peace. There is no clutter left in my mind to resist.

I think back and realize that the tee-shirts hanging high from wires in the tacky Plaka shops conveyed the message. Grey, black, white, they were the harbingers who brought the words of Nikos Kazantzakis from the rugged island of Crete to Athens to give me fair warning: "I hope for nothing. I fear nothing. I am free." I have been a stone, grey and rounded with time, without hard edges. I have been strong and determined, shutting the door to keep myself safe. I pushed and controlled and tried to keep the world at arm's length. Now I yearn to be the wind.

The cicadas are full-voiced now. Downstairs some of the writers are trying to untangle flight schedules, hotel reservations. I grab a cup of coffee and hurry back upstairs to my perch. I won't return to the village, the narrow streets. The gods claimed me, led me here to the *meltemi*. It blows at my back, roars and cajoles and hurls the shutters against our wall. *Meltemi* is wild. Untamable. A love that can't be contained or controlled or trapped inside a room.

I remember the night before at the taverna when Mary Jean asked, "Why do Greeks sing?" I leaned closer to listen to Virginia's answer. "It's because of the beauty. It sets your soul free. And your mind." If I write her words, can I claim them for my own? Can I let the *meltemi* blow through me? Can I laugh when I'm happy, cry when I'm sad?

Another gust of wind brings me back to my morning balcony, my cup of coffee—now cold. The church on the hillside is golden with the morning light. Colleen's white shirt and khaki pants struggle and flap, long since dry, pinned to the laundry rack. Grasshoppers have joined the chorus of cicadas as the sun warms the garden plots, olive trees, fig trees with yet unripe fruit.

I gather my cold coffee and return to Virginia's kitchen where a short while ago the counter was a cacophony of friends, peaches, halvah, coffee, sugar, honey, bread, biscotti and thick, sweet berry jam. The kitchen is empty. The counter spotless. All the clutter is gone, replaced with the pure tones of Amalia Rodriguez's voice bouncing off the stone floor from the stereo. Every blue-bottomed glass lined to dry on the counter, each one in perfect order; the white cups on the back of the sink; copper pots hung from the ceiling in the corner by the white lace curtains.

Virginia dances down the stairs, her hair wet from a shower, a white towel wrapped around her slender body. Virginia is my *meltemi*.

"I show you how to make the coffee," she offers. Though my knee makes my steps awkward, I spin, hop, turn across the stone floor while Virginia sings in French. That's exactly what I'll do. I'll dance. Sing. Listen. *I* will make coffee . . . and I will pass it on.

The Winds of Mesochori

M. J. PRAMIK

The knock at the weathered door startled the breakfast circle. It was Yiannis, Virginia's neighbor.

"Is Mary Jean here?" asked the quiet-spoken Greek gentleman. "I have found her passport blowing and tumbling in the wind." Yiannis' extended hand gently presented the thin blue book.

The gusty *meltemi*, an unusual wind for a Peloponnesian summer, had played with my paper identity along the dusty red clay road near the arched entry to Virginia's retreat. I had not yet missed this essential document, having just arrived the day before at a writers' workshop in the southern tip of Greece.

We had disembarked at the Vatika village of Mesochori on

a hot humid Monday afternoon. Traveling for five hours by freeway from Athens, then country roads to reach Neapoli, the van finally crawled past the gray, aging ruins of the Venetian fortress of Aghia Paraskevi. Upon arrival, I realized why my travel research had not found any mention of this mountainside hamlet. Mesochori, once an important contributor to Vatika's district government, hangs on the edge of a carved, virtually vertical hill. It watches over the growing town of Neapoli, centered on concave Neapolis Bay.

I had come to Greece searching for a respite to mend my tired spirit. My mother had died several months earlier and I needed some peace and solace from my grinding American life to continue the grieving process. I needed the space wherein to decide which memories to keep, which to discard. Friends offered comfort of sorts; they advised that each person must complete the first difficult, yet vital, year of mourning the loss of a mother to move on to the next stage of living.

My work responsibilities had granted me a few weeks off at the time to set family needs in order, but I turned to my daily frenzied work schedule to sidestep the void of holidays, my mother's first missed birthday, the reflex of telephoning every Saturday morning with the week's summary of news. My youngest child's college applications, auditions, and teenage rebellion had packed the year with further chaotic activity so that I could legitimately ignore any residual sadness. My aching muscles and listless spirit petitioned for a time alone near the seaside for cleansing and rest. An effusive Greek-American friend residing in Athens dangled a compelling offer of a writers' workshop near the southern seaside town of Neapoli.

Thus, I stand in the here and now of Mesochori with a kind stranger.

"*Efharisto*. Thank you. *Efharisto poli*," was my grateful reply in limping Greek. He had saved me days of delay at the U.S. embassy.

Yiannis, John in his adopted city of Vancouver, British Columbia, embraced my hand. He recalled how he had not returned to his birth village of Mesochori for sixty years. However, when vast changes in the global economy reached his Canadian engineering firm and forced his retirement, he and his wife decided to revisit these sunlit mountains.

"I felt at home. I had grown up in Mesochori and attended high school in Neapoli. I felt I belonged." Yiannis looked down at his weathered hands as he joined the group for coffee. He recounted his days as an engineer in the far western province of Canada. His engineering and architectural skills facilitated his building an exquisite white-walled, three-story home at the outer edge of Mesochori, where he lives with Mary, his wife, for six months each year.

As we continued in quiet conversation, Yiannis told of his memory loss, a topic always on his mind it seems. It's as if he keeps it front and center of his cerebral cortex, lest he forget himself.

"I remember the important things," he said almost in reverie. He remembers his love for his wife, his native land, his daughter and two dear grandsons. The thought of the latter brings a broad smile to his eyes. He remembers how to set tomatoes and zucchini in the red clay garden on the hillside in Mesochori each spring.

As he spoke, I began to remember. I, too, have experienced a memory loss. Following a traumatic divorce at a time of my own aging, I became a single parent unintentionally, then an orphan unexpectedly. At times, I search through the set synaptic pathways that were once so keen and thorough. I often do not find what I am looking for immediately. Then, days later, the face, the name, the flower, or the poem surfaces, as if to surprise me.

"I think my memory loss is from the world moving too fast, from the computers making things so jumbled at times." Yiannis' gaze connected with mine. I sat upright. That sentiment had often crossed the diffracting web that has become my mind.

Yiannis moved on to another connection.

"These winds are very unusual. They are more than the *meltemi.*" He reckoned that global warming has wreaked havoc with weather everywhere, even here in the sacred precinct that is southern Greece. He related his experience of the "disaster winds" that sped down from the north at one hundred miles per hour a few years ago and overturned boats in Neapolis Bay.

"I watched as it blew off the side of my garage here. It just sheared the wall," he recounted.

I returned to the night of our arrival. With temperatures well over 95 degrees Fahrenheit, a ferocious, swirling rain pounded the red-tiled roof of our retreat. The ill-tempered *meltemi,* rattled the worn unpolished shutters at their iron latches. Huddled inside the white walls, I felt each gust lunge up the precipitous hillside, as if an angry god determined to slay trees—olive and fig—and to uproot the chaparral not deeply embedded in the earth. Bending tightly, I held my knees close to form a ball. I imagined the trees trying to protect their fruits from this thieving wind. Where did the ubiquitous cicadas and grasshoppers seek shelter on such a night?

Leaves burst under the door, resembling multi-colored scorpions. Centipede-like creatures appeared on the hanging towels. Sparrows sang and cicadas rasped in rhythm despite the colossal drafts that blasted up the mountain from the waters below. Lying in the dense darkness, I waited for the squall to pass. For three days and nights I waited along with the tankers and boats anchored in Neapolis Bay, too timid to challenge Poseidon's lashes. It was as if this *meltemi* wanted all to know who controlled their travels.

The next day, a lull allowed a meditative amble around the mountainside villages of Mesochori, Faraklo, and Paradisi. At the lightened pace of Greek time, the gentle pace created a cavernous echo of thought. I imagined hearing voices from the hermits, the shepherds, the sailors, and their widows on the shore, who had wandered this land eons ago. Abandoned brown-gray stone corpses of ancient buildings lean comfortably against the whitewashed new limestone and marble structures that speckle the mountainside villages. Hiking through Mesochori and onward to the next town of Faraklo, I wondered what histories and myths lay buried in these empty structures without roofs and window frames without glass. These hollowed-out buildings raised the thought of my mother's unemptied bureau and my father's request to leave the clothes inside "because somebody may need them someday."

Angled some one thousand feet above the sea level town of Neapoli, Mesochori connects to civilization by a dirt road following challenging blacktop switchbacks not for the faint of heart. Wild cicadas scream during the sunlight hours and a lonely rooster punctuates random moments of the day. The white church of Christ's Transformation stands closed, damaged by an earthquake years ago. The nearby graveyard hosts twenty-seven tombs in the Greek Orthodox tradition. Several house husbands and wives who lived together for over half a century and now remain so in eternity.

Resting on the stairs behind the church, I begin to understand why a sojourn in Greece was so necessary at this time in my life. An accepting country with wide-open-armed people provides fertile ground for metamorphosis. I discover a cicada exoskeleton littering the ground. Would that it were so easy for us larger multi-celled creatures to shed a tiresome persona. Caught up in midlife, tumultuous changes, lost husbands, broken promises, departing parents, and children leaving home, the moment of transformation beckons. I seem to be in the process of reinventing myself in every moment, at times with nanometer transmutations, at others battered by a wild *meltemi*.

I carefully store my passport. I consider how to remember more of who I really am. The adventurous five-year-old, who challenged a small-town existence when the world seemed ever so big and exciting, remains somewhere at my core. As does the fresh college graduate who hitchhiked across the country to California at twenty-two because that place defined the edge of the world.

It was fitting that I lost my passport. Yet it was returned to me by a gentle man, who at another point on this planet, had experienced thoughts synchronous with mine. We met on a craggy hillside thanks to an unusual wind. These days have allowed me to reflect upon myself. Will I return a changed woman? Will I better process the loss of a mother, who I could not please, and change how I express my love for my children? They ask for unconditional love, *agapi*, the acceptance of their humanity, their missteps. My metamorphosis requires that I listen to a son's rap music, four-letter words and all, seeing that these songs parallel the music of the 60's. It demands valuing my middle child's painful mistakes, allowing her to take on a new luster like that of her all-encompassing smile. It means appreciating my eldest child's tenacity and elegance as she develops at her own pace. Shedding my brittle outer core will require creating the time to feel the Greek *parea*, to feel a sense of community, a time for friends.

Perhaps Yiannis is correct that the speed and frenetic nature of our Western existence prevent us from remembering the habits of kindness and love that spring spontaneously from the fully-present Greek. Like Yiannis, I feel more at home here. As I walk the road to Mesochori, I feel more alive.

Finding the time to change can be daunting at best. But sometimes life forces the issue as it has over my past few years. Here I watch several Greek women who daily manifest the courage to be themselves. Some days, I still feel like a leaf tossed in the wind in inelegant disarray. Other days, I feel like the wind itself.

Unnatural Tumbleweeds

On this barren slope, incessantly besieged by winds,
I used to race the bouncing tumbleweeds down
to the pebbled shore;
or, lying at the water's edge, I would wait for them to descend
and then, with a soccer-trained kick, I would send them
into the sea, toward new, wave-tossed journeys . . .

Beyond this rugged hill, across Persephone's meadow,
they would gather their shadow-growing bodies
and roll on unchartered paths.

Here, on this sacred field, I first spun my growing dreams.

And now, in this troubled Spring, on the same Aegean shore,
I turn my back to the once magic slope,
trying to block off, as in a nightmare, the new tumbleweeds—
plastic bags, billowing in the wind, descending on the littered shore.

For how long will Persephone return to bring her green Spring
on our choking Earth?

        – THANASIS MASKALERIS

Greeks Bearing Gifts

Joanna Biggar

><

A place unknown is a piece of a puzzle to be unlocked. Usually before entering completely new territory, I inform myself by reading—books, articles, travel pieces, poems. But heading for the very southern tip of the Peloponnese in the notoriously hot July of 2006, I found I was going to a village, Mesochori, found on no map, in a region, Vatika, also mysteriously absent from atlases and indexes. Clearly, my normal line of research would have to be revisited. I have always believed in the intertwining of character and place—and the charm of the unexpected—but could never have guessed what was to come. On my very first night in Vatika it not only rained, but the key to unlocking its myriad mysteries came to me not as a text, but as a kind of incarnation—in the figure of a beautiful woman in a diaphanous white dress.

Virginia is a small, lithe, deeply tanned woman beyond the reaches of age. Her short, dark hair is severely combed back from her face to reveal her black eyes and expressive brows; she is always dressed in her signature white; her brown arms are frequently adorned with silver bracelets; her feet are often bare. When she opens her mouth, she may speak in a gentle, animated voice, or she may sing in a huge, tremulous voice that seems to have its roots somewhere deep in the earth. When she moves, it may be with the quiet, tender efficiency of a mother, or it may be with the heart-stopping tempo of a dancer, pausing only to let the earth breathe. Since, except when asleep, she is always talking, singing, moving or dancing, the slight breeze of the zephyr seems to follow her movements. In her wake there is the feel of a poem.

On that first night in Vatika, in her small villa built into the rugged hills of Mesochori, I first came to understand something of her sense of hospitality. She greeted me with the warm hand and kisses that she offered to every newcomer, every stranger to her home, and then with the telling "thank you for coming" that instantly erased the very concept of stranger. She guided me to a cushion-lined banquette in her living room and sat down with me to explain how her friend Connie had persuaded her to take leave from her job in public relations for a television station in Athens to host a group of foreign writers.

"She talked about how you felt, how you behaved, and I felt as if friends were coming," Virginia recounted. "I was happy to give my heart and soul and whatever I have . . . I cannot be even a few minutes with people I don't feel well with [because] I take in both good and bad energy. I am open . . . If I feel it, I can do it."

The last sentence was a refrain I was to hear many times. It meant anything from cooking a superb multi-coursed meal, to singing cabaret-style for her friends, to swimming gloriously topless and free in the inviting sea, to dancing spontaneously in any taverna—or street—when the feeling came.

I had come to Greece, to this enchanted and mysterious place called Vatika, as a writing instructor. I had also come, as all travelers do, heavy with my own baggage. In particular, I came in mourning. My father had died less than a month before my departure. When asked to complete a sentence that began, "I came to Greece searching for _____," I completed it with the word "solace." For me, I knew that there would be solace in the act of teaching writing and in spending time in a community of writers. I imagined solace in the sheer beauty of Greece, a country I had once visited nearly half a life-time before. And I cherished the thought of sharing part of that experience with Doug, my husband of less than four years. But I could not have imagined how there, in that special quality of light and air, solace and soul would become the same thing. I could not have imagined how, after every surge of unbidden tears, the land itself would embrace and turn me back to the realm of the living, nor how the simplicity of joy becomes a balm beyond imagining. And at every turn, Virginia was there to lead me by the hand into that landscape.

When she was a small child, Virginia's family left the town of Neapoli—on the bay below Mesochori—for Brussels. "My father was a famous tailor," she explained, "and the mayor of Neapoli. So when some tourists came and saw how he did tailoring, they invited him to take a good job in Brussels, in the biggest *maison de couture*. He was a free spirit; he took risks . . . and in October he left by boat."

Soon Virginia and her mother followed, and within a week she was in what she calls a "magic world," of supermarkets and French schools and the fast lane of the city. Later the family would move to Paris, a place she still adores. "But Greece was the whole world when I was abroad," she said. "I never left Neapoli . . . I felt that anything new I saw I wanted to bring back to make their lives better. They, the people, wouldn't know much of the outside world except for the visitors who came with tales. The people were not rich and not poor, but fishermen, shopkeepers and many seamen. At that time mostly the women did not work."

She returned to Neapoli for the first time again at age seventeen and she experienced then, as now, how "the bay, the rocks, the flowers in the hills, the smells welcome me. I don't see the cement on the road, I see the ground. I see things the way they were, first through the past of my childhood, then through the deep past of archeology." While still a young woman, she married a pilot, and when the marriage ended early in divorce, she asked herself why. It was then she realized she had married him primarily because he was from Neapoli. The marriage was a way home.

Years later, stone by stone she built her magical villa in the hills, her whitewashed home with a red roof and white, shaded terraces, white walls and floors with beautiful red rugs and wall hangings, full of found objects—stones, dried flowers, shells—collected from the land and arranged with an artist's eye. One especially prized possession is a doorknob given her from her childhood home in Neapoli when the new owners were renovating. Attached to no door in particular now, perhaps it opens all doors that she wishes to remain open—the lock and key together. "In Athens, I protect myself," she declared. "Here I am free."

From our first encounter, Virginia presented me with that vision of freedom, and I saw Vatika through that lens. The dusty mountain roads, villages of stone houses, crumbling stone walls, and old women covered head-to-foot in black, the extravagant riots of flowers, the goats running wild over rocky hillsides, the heart-stopping vistas of the sea, the tavernas with octopus drying on racks in the sun. To be sure these were deeply rooted in a past—in archeology, to use Virginia's word. And to be sure, this was a place rich in history. There are remains of Neolithic inhabitants on the Bay of Neapolis, and a sunken city from the Mycenaean Age just off-shore. Surviving the wild weather at Cape Meleas, Odysseus sailed these waters to find Cyclops and Sirens and Circe on his long way back to Ithaka. Heroes from the Peloponnesian Wars, Romans, crusading Franks, Byzantines, Venetians, and Ottomans, all came and went—leaving legacies from the great walled city of Monemvasia to ruined castles on the hillsides—and for centuries mainly pirates ruled. Yet it is as if the land remembers them, but moved on, drawing on the rich loam of the past to cultivate the future. This is not the Greece one visits to explore ruins; this is the Greece one explores to find meaning in the living present.

One session I planned to teach in the writers' workshops was on myths and how, over time, their stories and purposes may be changed to fit modern situations. But even before getting to that workshop, I was learning the lesson for myself. From that first night in Mesochori, I was coming to see a different meaning to the ancient Greek adage—referring to Odysseus' trickery in giving a wooden horse filled with enemy soldiers to the Trojans—"Beware Greeks bearing gifts." Because for me, Greeks were bearing gifts all the time. Gifts of kindness, patience and tolerance for the foreigner who mangled the language by saying "*Kalamari*" (squid) or "*Kalamata*" (a kind of olive) meaning "*Kalimera*" (good morning), and "*Parakalo*" (please) instead of "*Efaristo*" (thank you). Gifts of helpfulness, laughter and conversation.

And none gave more than Virginia, for whom the art of giving is a kind of *raison d'être*. She could never sell space in her magical home for commerce any more than she would sell her magnificent voice for a living. They are meant only to be freely given. "If I feel it, I can do it." Thus she brings in found, natural or abandoned objects to remake them; thus she casts her net of gifts into the world.

In particular, I am thinking of the story she told about going into an old cemetery near her house and finding the grave of a woman with no living family. From the grave she knew the name was a Turkish surname, and though there has been ancient enmity between Greeks and Turks, they have also been neighbors and friends. For Virginia, all that mattered was that a human being not be forgotten. She found objects belonging to the dead woman that had been abandoned. Slowly, carefully, she picked up the things to repair them, to bring them into her own home to use, including several rugs which she washed in the sea to restore their color. She did this not because she needed more things, but so that the woman's memory, through her still-used objects, would return to and be honored by the living. This simple, loving act was also a special, if unintended, inspiration to me, a woman newly grieving her father.

There were, of course, so many others, beginning with Virginia's childhood memories, which like bouquets of flowers, I had gathered to myself. Like any life, hers was not one without sorrow, loss and tragedy, beginning with the moment of childhood when she was whisked out of Greece. But she had found within her—within her native Vatika—the Greek genius for self-repair and renewal with the simplicity of daily ritual, of dining, laughter, dancing. She had found the Greek way of bringing the past, and the dead, into the cycle of the living and the present. In this land where even the rocks seem able to sing, everywhere there is joy—and a long embrace that brings in even strangers who do not know the words. To me, this was the greatest gift of all.

Through the Trap Door

DOREEN WOOD

⟩⟨

Shards of a door opening flashed in my mind. As I tried to remember the nightmare that awoke me, the last trace of it vanished. I could see pale early light through my hotel window and could hear workers unloading boxes of fresh sardines and calamari from a truck on the other side of Apollonos Street. I was in Athens, Greece.

My expedition was just beginning. I'd planned the trip months earlier and had been looking forward to the experience. At sixty-three years old, I'd had some health problems and recently spent several days in the hospital with pneumonia. For a while, I wasn't sure I could make the trip. A gnawing dread sat in the pit of my stomach at the prospect of traveling by myself to Athens. A myriad of imagined disasters lurked in my mind. I could lose my purse and my money. I'd be alone for four days before joining my group.

Part of me sensed that somehow I would manage and I was determined to work through my fear, step by step. I remembered a trip my family took one winter to Yosemite National Park in California. Taking a shuttle bus from the valley to the top of Badger Pass, our daughter went off to the lifts to downhill ski, while my husband, young son and I began a trek into the woods on our cross-country skis. Finding a sunny meadow, we undid our backpacks, perched on a rock, and enjoyed our lunches. But the sky was darkening, so I told them I was going to ski back down to the lodge. Only minutes after I was on the trail, heavy snow began to fall, thunder growled, and lightning streaked through the trees. The zigzag flashes raced around me, sizzling in their intensity. I knew that my steel ski poles were lightning rods. My knees began to shake and knock against each other. But I kept pressing forward, one ski after the other, and successfully made it down the mountain path.

I thought of my ski trip as I arrived alone in Athens and checked myself into the modest Omiro Hotel in the center of the Plaka district. Dimitri was the afternoon desk clerk, a grizzled man past retirement age, cigarette smoke curling upwards from the ashtray at his side. In the ensuing days, I learned that Dimitri's bark disguised his benevolence.

During my second night at the Omiros, I lay awake all through the night, my body confused by the ten-hour time difference. At five a.m., I showered and emerged into the hotel lobby. Dimitri, on night duty, rose and made me a steaming cup of filtered coffee from the tiny kitchen behind the desk. Stepping back into the kitchenette, he returned with a delectable piece of lemon cake on a paper doily. He ordered me to eat it, telling me that it was from his home.

Contemporary Athens was more about the here and now than the ancient classics, although wherever I turned, the Parthenon loomed large overhead. I spent hours wandering through the narrow streets and alleys of the Plaka, dozens of motorbikes, cars and taxicabs constantly zooming by, making deafening noises, spewing acrid fumes.

On Mitropoleos street, near the massive Mitropoleos Cathedral, I came upon a tiny chapel, now dwarfed by four-story modern buildings. I found that its ochre walls and marble doorframe concealed a dim interior illuminated by dozens of tapering prayer candles. I watched people come in to pray in silence. I thought about myself alone in a strange city. I thought of friends alone at home and lit a candle for all of us.

As I sat in the Omiro hotel breakfast room on my last full day in Athens, I spotted a fresh, open face and on impulse, walked over to her, and asked, "Are you Gail Strickland?"

"Well, yes I am," she responded. "And you must be Doreen! I've just flown in and am already having such adventures! And have you seen the nest of newborn swallows here on the window ledge?"

Meeting Gail gave me an intimation of the magic that was to come in the following ten days. She and I spent the day talking and shopping the stalls of the Plaka and Monastiraki. She is a grounded, sensitive woman, and I felt her healing sensitivity as I told her my fears about this trip.

By late afternoon, the sky had perceptibly darkened. Papers scuttled into narrow corners. My bare arms and shoulders became cool. Shopkeepers pulled their wares to indoor safety. Gail and I sat within the shivering tarpaulin of a bar. She sipped her fragrant, anise-flavored ouzo. I decided against the potent drink, feeling no need to filter the silver-gold shards of crooked lightning. Thundering skies opened and sheets of rain surrounded us, but we stayed dry.

Twenty-four hours later, our group of writers traveled south by van for five hours, through hillside villages studded with whitewashed, red-roofed houses until we reached our destination, Vatika. The trip was mostly in silence. I eyed the others somewhat balefully. One writer had completed a novel based in Delphi in the third century B.C. Several others were widely read in Greek mythology. How was I going to measure up? I carried a little handbook of Greek mythology in my suitcase but my historical knowledge was of the most general sort. I felt like an ignorant fool, wishing that I'd studied the classics instead of majoring in scientific subjects.

Our home for the next ten days was two narrow, whitewashed structures, one the main house, and the other, a smaller guesthouse, both built into the rocky mountainside. On the first evening, our captivating host, Virginia, served us wine and Greek delicacies as we sat on the terrace, looking east at the turquoise Bay of Neapolis far below. The dry, wild wind, the infamous *meltemi*, had blown in, followed by pelting rain. Eventually, clutching my roommate

Catherine, I slipped and stumbled along a rocky walkway, down steps that at first glance seemed impossible and precarious, to our stone-floored lower-level suite.

Our second evening, we traveled higher on narrow roads to the village of Faraklo. In the misty light of an almost full moon, houses huddled around the square of the Evangelistria. A mountain spring poured from a rocky enclave where villagers had gathered for centuries to fill their jugs and exchange news of the day, and where a very lively cicada gleefully poured out his cut-glass hiss. We looked down on the islands of Kythira and Elafonisos silhouetted in the bay.

Around midnight, I was back in my downstairs suite. It had two long, padded sectionals for sleeping, a small crescent-shaped fireplace, and wall shelves filled with local *objets d'art*. I donned my long white nightgown. I could hear my colleagues singing and dancing above me in the living room. Looking around, I was intrigued by a sturdy wooden ladder that extended from the stone floor to the ceiling. I wondered where I would end up if I climbed those tempting rungs. I hesitated, but couldn't resist. At the top, I pushed hard against what appeared to be a trap door. Suddenly, it gave way. The floor above opened up, and triumphantly I rose into the kitchen. My fellow writers gaped at me in astonishment as I floated into the living room in my long white gown.

Virginia was teaching everyone to tango. I closed the trap door tightly and joined the group. No longer afraid of illness, traveling alone, ignorance, or being accepted by the group, I danced and twirled with new-found confidence and joy.

Contemporary Goddesses

Ann Kathleen Ure

Greek women don't sweat; they glow. The old saying seems to apply to these women who appear to move through the world seemingly effortlessly. I do not.

I have come to Greece in the summer of 2006 to join a group of American travel writers. After just a few hours in Athens, I make my way to the Acropolis. And, in just one more hour, I convince myself that all Greek women share four unique qualities. Each possesses dark eyes, olive skin, thick brown hair, and the ability to scale mountains in delicate, high-heeled sandals.

Alongside these modern-day Persephones and Demeters, I feel like an Amazon. Amongst all the tourists at the Acropolis, they appear to be skipping up the mountain path accessorized only with pastel-colored clutch bags and flip-up cell phones. My climb is laborious and sweat-soaked. I stop often to admire the view, which we all know is code for "in my efforts to stifle my panting, I am a mere ten steps away from passing out."

In contrast to the petite, seemingly winged sandals that adorn the feet of the young Greeks, my feet are shod—rather like a horse's—in thick white sweat socks and sneakers. And the climb is made more arduous by the canvas tote bag I'm schlepping. It's weighted down with two guidebooks, a Euro-stuffed wallet, sunscreen, bug repellant, two cameras, a flashlight and back up batteries. Over-encumbered as I am, witnesses may assume that my visit to the Acropolis is a brief diversion from my real trek which began in the Balkans and will conclude in Istanbul.

Observing the Greek women ascend the mountain, I conclude that they have been given special powers that elude me. I am quite sure that the ensuing week—to be spent in the city of Piraeus and the Vatika region of southern Greece—will confirm my suspicion that I am among contemporary goddesses.

When Kristina, a twenty-first century Aphrodite, enters the Piraeus apartment where we will stay for two nights, I feel like I've been slingshot straight back to high school. Tall, lean, tan, perky—and with long brown hair, tight designer jeans, and a low-cut tee-shirt—she is everything I once wanted to be. She speaks of juggling two jobs and striving to succeed in a male-dominated Athens. But at that moment of first impressions, all I hear is "Blah,

blah, blah. Could I be any cuter? And, by the way, doesn't my ass look tiny in these jeans?"

The oh-so-perfect Kristina leads our group around the perimeter of the Piraeus harbor to a popular fish taverna. There are few diners at nine o'clock, but a large wait-staff of teenage boys in varying colors of tight polo shirts. Three follow her to our table, tripping over themselves like puppies. The others follow her, too, but only with their eyes.

Kristina is polite with Angelos, the head waiter, but rather brusque with her boy toys. Yiannis, the one in the pink polo shirt, cannot contain his feelings for her and hovers around our table most of the evening. Clearly he hopes that she will find herself with a need and that he may be able to fill it. Between the Greek salad and squid courses he sucks up all the courage he can muster and whispers in her ear.

"I got your phone number from the reservation book. May I call you sometime?"

"You may not!" she replies sharply, and with a flick of her wrist sends him away with his puppy tail tucked between his legs.

Over the course of the evening, we learn that Kristina is more than a Greek boy's fantasy date and a pretty face. She is dedicated to her work. And she has set ambitious career goals which she feels are being thwarted by her male bosses. Her day job is interim director for a prestigious Athens firm. And several nights per week she moonlights, via the miracle of technology, for a firm in the United States.

Kristina complains that her macho Athens boss is very pleased with her performance but is reluctant to slot her into the director's role—something that the American women at the table can relate to.

She voices her extreme dissatisfaction with his stalling, in Greek, *"Efages to gaidero ke emine i oura."*

We Americans nod our heads empathetically, assuming that she has represented feminists everywhere by stating that the best man for the job is often a woman. However, when asked to translate her declaration, she haughtily states, "You've eaten the donkey and left the tail."

I turn to see one of my tablemates silently mouth *"Huh?"* then ask Kristina to translate her translation for us. The explanation that follows has nothing to do with her gender or her sex appeal. Rewording the translation of her maxim, Kristina quietly but firmly states that her boss would be a fool to let her go before she can finish the job she's begun. And at that moment I know that goddess Kristina and I have more in common than I'd originally thought.

In Vatika, Dionysus appears to me as a contemporary Greek Auntie Mame named Connie. Born and raised in San Francisco and of Greek descent, Connie relocated to Greece at the age of twenty-nine and never looked back. Now, as a friend and guide, Connie delivers us to new experiences, enhancing them every step of the way with her warmth, energy, and personal charisma.

My first meeting with Connie was in Paris a year earlier. She swept into our tiny apartment, set down her luggage, and—one by one—pulled us to her for hugs and sets of European air kisses. Grabbing up diminutive Linda, a friend for life she hadn't seen in over a year, she cried *"Agapi moo!"* This endearment (my love, in

English) became a Connie trademark. We hear it more frequently now that we're in Greece. I've been *agapi-mooed* by Connie's friends and family, and even by a Neapoli cab driver. But it continues to carry extra weight when it comes from the goddess herself.

Dionysus, like Connie, was a fan of the grape. But neither Dionysus, then, nor Connie, now, are reliant upon spirits to live fully and in the present. The Dionysian gift of wine is, they say, more of a catalyst for the rest of humanity to take a load off; let our hair down; get over ourselves; and otherwise engage all our senses in a "state of holy intoxication."

As everyone in our group is to discover, being with Connie is slightly intoxicating, with or without the alcohol. Being with Connie is like being admitted to the high school "in crowd" again, or perhaps for the first time, for those of us who are very late bloomers. She's the most popular girl in the senior class. And if you're lucky, like me, she'll draw you into her circle.

I imagine myself as Connie and realize that, at best, I display her qualities in small measure. It's the scale, really. I can be witty and engaging, but no one has ever likened me to Auntie Mame or even to Rosalind Russell. Connie *is* the party. The room is full with her in it. To be with Connie is to have the most fun, sing and dance the longest, laugh the loudest.

At the dinner parties I host at home we usually fold up the tent by 11:00 o'clock. Goddess Connie would be putting out appetizers at the same hour and have dinner planned for midnight, charades at two, then an ocean swim beneath the moon and the stars at four. My guess is that many of her friends do not go home til the next afternoon, or even the following Monday. Some may never go home at all.

As the goddess most closely associated with liquid spirits, Connie pours liberally and challenges mere mortals like me to keep up with her. Always the loser in each of these contests, I now discover that she's been watering down her wine with club soda for years. She's not the one who needs the alcohol to get herself onto the dance floor. I am. So she prods me along to a place I want to go. And if I find it exciting, and safe, I'll likely get there next time with a little less wine and a little more soda, too.

On my best days, and especially here in Greece surrounded by so many friends, I see myself becoming increasingly extroverted and willing, in my own way, to draw others into the circle as she does. Perhaps a little of the goddess Connie is rubbing off on me after all.

Goddess number three, Virginia, is our wise Athena, and she knocks my socks off at first glance. Elegant cropped hair, flawless bronze skin, a dancer's body, and clothed only in a white wrap, she is exquisite. The wrap is something we will see many times over the ensuing week— but never in the same composition. Like Linus' blanket that morphs from a burnoose to scarf to toga, Virginia's wrap is little more than a scrap of white gauze that is, at times, a bathrobe, a mini dress, and a shawl. Even ancient Greeks known for their textiles and tapestries would be impressed with Virginia's style. How does she do so much with so little?

Virginia's role with us in Vatika is mother hen. She tends to all our needs: dishing out meals, wisdom, consolation, and tango lessons in equal measure. We all aspire to be Virginia. If she were to take on a new vocation, it could be as a spiritual guide—or head mistress at a boot camp for goddess wannabes.

Not surprisingly, it's not just the women who are drawn to Virginia. She is the designated arranger of reservations, taxis, and other appointments that must be made during our time here, because there isn't a man in Greece who can say no to her. Unlike my own experience of flailing and failing to secure a taxi in Athens, Neapoli cabbies will make the fifteen-minute drive up the mountain and navigate the rock-covered dirt path just to catch a glimpse of her. They come to pick up the American writers for a day-trip but must invariably park, toot their horns, and call out *"Kalimera, Virginia!"* to see her smile before they'll load us into the cars and head back down the mountain. When goddess Virginia herds us into a restaurant, men pop out of nowhere to greet her—or, more accurately, to devour her with wolf-like appreciation.

Virginia's lovely appearance is not dependent upon makeup. She simply doesn't need it. In Greece I don't wear makeup either. I'm not going without because my blotchy skin has been evened out after repeated exposure to the sauna that is Greece. And it's not that supplemental measures wouldn't enhance my looks. It's that any eyeliner I apply at nine in the morning will have slid down to form a black mustache by noon. I've packed up my lipstick in favor of lip balm, too. The only thing worse than an eyeliner mustache would be the mustache above my lips paired with a champagne pink Clinique soul patch below.

It's been an effort to identify any cracks in Virginia's veneer.

She is a woman of substance—to a degree that could be intimidating were she not so open and kind. She is at once a superb cook, an interior designer, a TV producer, a chanteuse, a dancer, a mother, a fashion statement, a philosopher, a consummate gardener, and a hostess who speaks five languages. I don't stack up particularly well alongside Virginia, though I assume that there must be some way that the chasm between us can be bridged.

And so I look for a common denominator. It reveals itself to me on our fourth day in Vatika when I decline the day trip planned for our group and spend a day, alone, with Virginia in our Mesochori home. We eat lunch together in her kitchen, in front of the open window that overlooks the valley leading to the Mediterranean Sea. Between bites of *mizithra* cheese and honey she tells me more about her life and personal philosophy. While delicately nibbling her lunch, Virginia spies a common pest, now an arch-enemy, that alights on our honey. It is one of many houseflies buzzing about in the midday heat, a constant irritant in this beautiful home with many windows, no screens, and the constant movement of writers in and out of doors.

Virginia's sophisticated façade cracks as she grabs a fly swatter beneath the counter and begins to swipe at the intruders. She is overtaken by a focused frenzy and eliminates one, two, three flies in quick succession. At last! This is my first glimpse of the mortal Virginia! I take up a second swatter and join her in the hunt with a surprising rate of success. Only minutes before I was *Grasshopper* at the feet of the goddess master. Now we're just a couple of gals cleaning house, dashing wildly from room to room in our efforts to protect our meal of Greek honey and cheese from these unwelcome winged interlopers. Finally, I've discovered an arena in which I can compete.

Our last night in Mesochori is celebrated with local family, friends, and neighbors under a glorious full moon. I take this opportunity to ask several of the male guests what makes Greek women so special. Not one mentions appearance, sex appeal, or the ability to drink their dinner companions under the table. Instead, they tell me that Greek women are strong and confident. The secret, they say, is that Greek women are comfortable in their own skins.

Pondering this information and surveying the scene of both Greek and American women who have bonded through their shared experiences, I realize that all of them are self-aware, confident and strong. And so am I! This fact is driven home when each of us Americans is bestowed with the name of an ancient Greek goddess or muse. Now Euphrosyne, I am cited for my good cheer, mirth, and merriment. I am a lover of song, and a darling of harmony.

After another sip of Dionysian wine, I gaze down at my feet and envision them in the delicate winged sandals that have graced the feet of goddesses old and new. These sandals fit me just fine, as do the sneakers and sweat socks that I wore at the beginning of my journey. Either way, I am a contemporary and true goddess. I've got it all.

Penelope and the Suitors

She had heard the whispers:
fish-tailed maidens
with nets of gold hair,
those sirens, their bitch calls piercing
his ears, painted hands strumming
his legs
and Circe. Ah, Circe,
wild young body dancing to calypso eyes,
that one, she'd heard, had lasted a year.
But only Helen's face
oval goddess beauty
that he had looked upon
haunted her

and her heart, slow constricted fist beyond the leap of yearning,
    stopped its beating.

Now, they said, he was dead.

For the first time in twenty years she laughed, twenty years of rock
island, stone, sea, swells of waiting.
Now he was near and those who could not follow his wake said he
was dead, those who could not tell dying from coming.

At last near coming home,
and the waves pulled back from the beach
like parted lips, like
hands running over hips,
rounded still, and she laughed
again knowing how the gods and suitors
wet their tongues.

Hair to waist, laced with silver
precious metal, like gold
on the looking-glass
where her face, smooth and finely laced,
finely colored from
twenty summers' sun was,
she knew, lovely.

So, what had he heard?

If he knew her, he would know
she did not remain untouched,

not by the sinewy black one
who loved her like the night,
or the fisherman with the wise beard
casting his net of stories
about her, rubbing her back,
or the philosopher who thought best
with his slender fingers,
or that young artist with Vulcan eyes,
all like the seasons, her weave of patches
a coverlet to cover
the marriage bed.
That was what they came to.

Still she dreamed Odysseus,
closed her eyes to see him
wearing those twenty years.
But she saw only his likeness,
Telemachus, the son,
beauty in his fierce and tender
restlessness,
the boy left behind, the guard
charged by men
to do what no man can:
Separate a woman from her desire.
Still she waited, had waited,
waited and wanted
husband, blood-mate,

twin of the inner mirror whose likeness only knew the holier
  longings of love. Then he came. Strong-chested, broad-armed,
  steeled in beard and bone.

Did he know at last what this journey had been for?

He saw her first, her eyes
the lissome blue his glance once
skated over,
mirrors on a pristine lagoon.
Now, around them, little creases,
terrain,
a holding place
before plunging
into the deep sea.
You are the most beautiful, he thought.
Yes, she smiled.
Come in

— JOANNA BIGGAR

Yiayia

CHRYSA TSAKOPOULOS

ᐳᐠ

"What will your mother-in-law think? She'll throw you out of her house!" I was twelve at the time; mother-in-laws were still a long way off.

"Greek is very important!" my yiayia (Greek for grandmother) roared. Her confidence in her conviction matched that of a campaigning politician.

But she wasn't a politician, she was a statesman. Towering over me at 5'3" in a long skirt and well-worn Ferragamo shoes, her opinions about life, men, and tank tops flowed freely from painted lips. Lonely struggles and suppressed tears compressed the once-full mouth. Sorrows were hidden behind Bordeaux colored lipstick. The same color brightened her cheeks, as she saw no difference between lipstick and blush. Rubbing bits of lipstick on her cheeks filled the creases and lines that came along with wisdom gained from personal battles fought and challenges conquered.

Her long nose served more for passing judgment than discerning scent. A life-long allergy sufferer, her sense of smell had dulled, but my yiayia would not think of letting one of her features go to waste.

"Look at her," she gasped at me one Sunday morning at church. "In the house of God without nylons!"

"It's July!" I fretted, feeling the sweat running down my stockings.

"No excuse! Women no respect anything! All they do is walk with strappy shirts and boobs!" Then up went the nose in indignation. "No class! Always be classy, then you succeed!"

Her eyes were her greatest attribute. Once clean-cut ovals, the skin began to hang heavy around her eyelids. The shape of her eyebrows was thick, though sparsely filled by hairs. But her dark brown eyes blazed from deep inside. When staring into them, pride, love, and compassion revealed themselves. Those eyes surveyed the world, and watched closely over those she loved, yet within them lay memories that she rarely, if ever, mentioned.

We were both named "golden blossom." Chrysanthy comes from the word chrysanthemum. The flower is famous for blooming in the fall and for its long life. I was the keeper of her name and in return she was my guardian angel.

I needed a guardian angel, for I was always scared senseless of the dark. The creeping shadows that slithered along the walls were not my desired roommates. They filled the room and almost choked me. Only Yiayia was able to chase them out. She would sleep beside me, snoring like a steam engine: the most comforting sound in the world when ghosts are around. She never sang lullabies or told me stories of princesses and dragons on faraway shores. Instead, her heavy, fearless breathing was enough to lull me into slumber. This went on until I was about twelve. Then we moved and I found myself sleeping alone.

"Don't be afraid my mermaid, I will always be near you."
Yiayia moved into the room next door and we shared the bathroom. I could still hear her snore.

My new bedroom also served as a classroom. Konstantina, a brilliant and wonderful Greek language teacher had just arrived from Greece.

"I don't do homework!" I announced on the first day of lessons. She just stared at me; heaven knows what ran through her mind.

"Okay," she responded skeptically.

In time, simple noun declensions and verb conjugations evolved into complex sentence structures and essays. Greek was not just a link to my heritage, but a fabulous code language. Opinions and comments could be publicly exchanged, yet not publicly understood. Yiayia took full advantage of my newly acquired foreign lexicon, not just for commentary, but recollection as well.

Experiences in World War II provided fertile fodder for storytelling. "When the Germans attacked Piraeus, they put a special alarm to signal for bombs," Yiayia slowly recalled half in English, half in Greek. Her father had warned his three children—Kostas, Yiannis, and Chrysoula—to stay off the busses in the Greek port of Piraeus at all times. "I was so young, so young." The alarm signaling the German Luftwaffe attack sounded, and Kostas and Yiannis desperately searched for their little sister, only to find her chasing a bus filled with her schoolmates. The boys quickly ran after my yiayia and caught her in their arms. She struggled against their firm grasp, but they did not let go. Suddenly a bomb exploded. Yiayia lifted her eyes to see the bus with her beloved friends blown to pieces in the middle of the street.

"They all die on the bus," Yiayia choked, tears flowing over the creases on her cheeks. I sat motionless, biting my lips in order to contain the tears brimming in my eyes. Although the story deeply touched me, I felt guilty knowing that my heart had never suffered so greatly. I could not imagine losing my classmates that way—to drunk driving accidents maybe, but blown-up busses, not very likely.

With due respect to her class and upbringing, Yiayia was no saint. For her, the notion of "turning the other cheek" signaled defeat. She believed in retaliation. When she was about sixteen, she liked a boy named Stephanos. He was handsome, but an "S.O.B.— Sweet Old Boy," she clarified. "He was very bad with me, and I say 'Enough!'" A year passed. Then, one day Yiayia met the former flame in the middle of the street. "I tell him I miss him and to meet me on Saturday in front of the church." Stephanos eagerly agreed and on Saturday afternoon arrived at the church in Piraeus, only to be met by my Yiayia and Pappou's wedding party. "He deserves it," Yiayia maintained. "Stupid, stupid boy."

In her later years, multiple mini-strokes claimed Yiayia's command of the English language. She and I communicated in Greek. It was during this period that I learned the most about her life.

She hardly ever spoke of my grandfather. He was handsome in the photographs I had seen, but the picture of him in my mind was concocted of those images and snippets of stories that I had heard from my mother and my aunts. One day, Yiayia decided to tell me a little bit about him.

"I met Tony when I was sixteen. He was a handsome Greek American from San Francisco. His parents were from Faraklo. During World War II, he was stationed in Naples, Italy with the U.S. Navy. He came to Greece before returning to America. The whole village was excited that Yiannis' son had come home. I had curlers in my hair," she continued, shyly batting her eyes and putting her little hand next to her head in order to show me the exact placement of the rollers, "and I saw him from inside my house." My Pappou (Grandfather) laid eyes on Yiayia and was instantly smitten.

"Be careful of that one," some of the village elders warned him when they heard of his attraction. "She's crazy! She goes alone to the movie theatre!" In the mid 1940's, that was indeed unusually bold. But when Yiayia turned eighteen, my Pappou returned to Greece just to marry her.

Turret's syndrome also took its toll on my Yiayia. Her physical and psychological condition worsened every day. She grew increasingly forgetful and ill-tempered. At night I would hear her vomiting in our bathroom, struggling to come to terms with her illness. Sometimes I would walk up to the closed door on my side and press my face against it, hoping that the torture would stop. "Lord," I prayed, "please, please help her." Although she never knew it, I often stood beside her as she slept, hoping that in some way my silent tears could soothe her body. I feared the world. But even more, I feared my own incapacity to face it alone.

On a Monday evening in late April of 2004, Yiayia and I were together at a dinner at California State University in Sacramento honoring her late husband.

"You come in San Francisco for the weekend. They play Tchaikovsky's operas!"

"Yes, Yiayia," I answered excitedly, "I'll come to San Francisco this weekend, I promise."

The following day, Yiayia suffered a massive stroke, and on Thursday night she joined her mother and husband and left all those who loved her here on earth. I kept my last promise to her. That weekend I drove with my family to the city. We dressed her in her finest suit, the black and silver one she wore to opening night at the opera.

The day of the funeral, I could not even tell what planet I was on. My wet eyes, irritated by salt and stung by misery, tried to focus on the blurry casket.

The day after Yiayia died, my father had approached me and suggested that I say something at the luncheon after the funeral.

"Say something?" I slowly annunciated, hardly able to control my mouth.

That night in my room, I stared blankly at the notebook in front of me. What could I say? I had so many fond memories and funny stories to tell, but at that moment they did not seem sufficient to express my love, or loss.

Suddenly, I realized that the greatest effect Yiayia had on me, *was* me! I was the way I was because of her immense influence on my character. In my eulogy, I spoke of the most important things she taught me. I recalled the elegant authority of orchids in making a room beautiful, and the affects of ouzo in providing sweet dreams. I also reiterated the importance of diamonds to a girl, and nylons to a woman. I realized that although she was not with me physically, she would always be within me.

After I spoke, I returned to my seat at the table and reached for my purse. I opened it and pulled out a small card that all of the guests had received upon entering the church. On it was a poem entitled "Free." The first line read "Don't cry for me 'cause I am free." I knew that my Yiayia was free; I felt it. Immeasurable pain was accompanied by limitless gratitude that I was able to love and be loved by such a wonderful woman.

Now, years later, I always smile when I pass the church where she was married in Piraeus, and I always make sure that my shirt covers my stomach. And even in the almost unbearable heat of a Neapoli summer she still tells me, "My mermaid, if you go to the church, put on your nylons!"

Pathway to Paradise

BARBARA J. EUSER

⤳

We were heading for *Paradisi*—Paradise. Remnants of rain-drops dripped from the eucalyptus trees as we started walking. My daughter Piper and I had spent all day indoors, confined by rain and wind. Now, late afternoon, a window of opportunity appeared. The rain stopped; the wind died down. Closing the black iron gate behind us, we turned right and head-ed upstream. That is, our imprecise instructions were to walk in the dry riverbed underneath the first bridge, then head up. There was nothing natural about this riverbed. It had been paved in concrete, and the banks were not crumbling earth, but solid stonework.

We skirted puddles that had accumulated in concrete depressions. A car was parked in the riverbed under the bridge, a substitute carport. Clearly flash floods were not expected here. A narrow path led from the riverbed up to the street. Was that our route? We had no map or hand-drawn chart, just a few verbal instructions. We walked a bit further, discovered a large side creek entering our riverbed and returned to the narrow path. As we climbed the short pitch, our running shoes clung to the mud.

Piper spotted the symbol: a red circle inside a white square. That must mean we were on the hiking trail. Or at least *a* hiking trail. In fact, we were back on the paved road. Why had we bothered to walk in the riverbed when we could have just walked up the road? We had simply followed instructions, with no understanding of the geography. Now we see through the mirror dimly.

Apple trees blossomed along both sides of the road. Without realizing it, we had left Neapoli and were walking uphill through the countryside. Houses spaced out, surrounded by olive trees, a few fig trees, roses beginning to bloom.

Piper strode purposefully, her long legs carrying her at a pace I could barely maintain. She is three inches taller than I am. She is stronger, too.

Twenty years ago, I carried her on my back, a baby in an aluminum-framed carrier with a canvas seat. During a long hike, sometimes she would fall asleep, her head bobbing against the back of my neck. Other times, she would get impatient with her means of conveyance. She would stand on the aluminum crossbar and pull my hair. White blond ringlets have turned to dark blond waves of shoulder-length hair. Her blue eyes still sparkle with mischief. But today the mischief is tempered with a degree of understanding.

A dog barked at us. We looked down into a yard of deep, churned mud. The dog was standing in the only dry place—on the side of a twenty-gallon metal drum. The drum was lying on its side in the mud and had been opened at one end to create a crude doghouse. The dog was chained to the barrel. The chain clanged as he struggled to maintain his balance, to keep from slipping off the rounded barrel side. His barks sounded like cries for help. But there was nothing we could do.

The hillsides around Neapoli appear sparsely vegetated, until one walks through them. Rough bushes and high weeds force one to stick to a path. But there are many paths to choose from in Vatika. Some of them follow dirt roads that turn into tracks. And some of them disappear completely, from lack of regular maintenance. I had seen trail symbols painted on rocks along the way to Mesochori, Faraklo, Aghia Paraskevi and La. Not so many years ago, donkeys laden with supplies plied up and down the rocky paths, crisscrossing the countryside.

After a mile or so, we came to an intersection. A dirt track turned off to the left, while the paved road continued. We saw our first trail sign: a stick-bodied hiker with a backpack and a walking stick on a small red placard. It read Δ 3 *Paradisi* 2.8 km. So we were on trail number 3 and we were on the right track! We turned left.

Within two minutes we stood befuddled. We had walked out of civilization, past the country houses with their wide gardens. We were in the midst of an untamed landscape. The track petered out in an olive grove. A streambed coming down the hillside seemed to be the only route. Would the walking route to Paradise follow a streambed?

Why not? Are there not four rivers in the gardens of Paradise? They flow with wine, water, milk and honey. The fountain of everlasting life is where they converge in the center of the garden. I have heard that is the description of Paradise in the Koran. And the charbagh gardens of Moghul India are laid out according to that design. Piper and I could not tell which of the four rivers we were in. Although the bed was wide, filled with smooth, worn stones, it was empty.

Around a bend, we came upon a square stone house. Two rows of olive trees stood like sentinels, marking this small plot of a former home. The stone terraces were intact, but, though the house appeared solid, the roof was gone. The doors and window frames gaped open, empty. Where had the residents gone?

I imagined myself living in that house. I could see the roof covered in red tiles with upturned corners. The window and doorframes, the door and wooden shutters were painted deep ocean blue. I imagined laboring with my husband building those stone terraces—one rock at a time. The rocks were heavy. Each one had to be carried from the field to the wall, then lifted into place, then worked into the final scheme. As we worked, we were drenched in sweat. It poured down my face, along my neck. But carrying a heavy stone, I couldn't wipe away the sweat. It stung my eyes. Course by course, we built the terrace wall.

Three terraces rose above the creek bed. I knew what labor and love had gone into building each one of them. I saw the fruit trees planted close to the house, the olive grove spread out along the terraces.

I imagined myself sitting on the doorstep, deciding where to plant the lemon trees, the pear trees. I chose an especially sunny spot for the fig tree. Outside the kitchen door, I planted herbs—mint and oregano. We built an arbor for the grape vines, establishing a spot to sit in the shade.

My dream ended. As Piper and I walked past the homestead, it returned to its actual condition, abandoned and left to ruin.

The streambed twisted and turned. The trail symbol, the red circle in a white square, was painted on a rock here, a stone wall there.

We passed another abandoned homestead, then another. A metal pipe crossed the dry streambed, spanning from one bank to the other, well above our heads. Water sprayed from a leak in a pipe joint. That was where the water in the stream had gone! Somewhere above us, the stream had been diverted into a pipe. Presumably, the pipe carried the water to a point where it was put to use. Maybe it was being used to irrigate the olive groves that still populated the multiple terraces.

After we passed under the pipe with its artificial waterfall, the streambed became more difficult to negotiate. We jumped from boulder to boulder, continuing our ascent. I followed Piper's lead, giving thanks I could.

A week earlier, Piper had been on her spring break from the American University in Cairo where she was studying for a semester.

She and a group of friends had traveled in backpacking, hostelling, student style from Egypt to Jordan, then into Israel to visit Tel Aviv and Jerusalem. I had expressed concern when she told me of their plans to go into Israel. The chronic terrorist attacks against unarmed civilians claim so many victims there. I could not bear for her to be among them. She emailed from Jerusalem to tell us that she and her friends had left the bus station in Tel Aviv twenty-four hours before it was bombed. Eight people died.

After several days in Jerusalem, she and her friends tried to enter Syria, but were turned back. They retraced their route through Jordan and into Egypt and decided to relax for a couple of days at the seaside resort of Dahab. On the day of their departure from Dahab, there were two busses to Cairo, one at 2:30 p.m. and one at 10:00 at night. Piper was inclined to take the night bus, but her friends preferred to get back to their dorm at a reasonable hour. So the group left Dahab in the afternoon. At 7 p.m. that evening, three bombs exploded in Dahab, one at the restaurant where Piper and her friends had eaten the day before and would have probably eaten again that evening. Twenty-three people died in the blasts.

Piper had come to Greece for the final days of her spring break to spend time with me in a secure environment. There are no guarantees of safety anywhere, but Piper had been spared twice, by increasingly narrow margins. In'ch Allah, God willing, I was clambering over boulders, hiking behind her up a streambed in Vatika.

A trail sign indicated a right turn, out of the streambed onto a narrow path through a weed-choked field. Again we passed stone terraces, still planted in olive trees, then a roofless stone house. A short flight of concrete stairs took us to a paved road. Red placards with stick-figured hikers directed us to Faraklo in one direction, or back the way we had come to Neapoli.

It started to rain. Piper and I stood under a broad-leafed mulberry tree and shared some almonds I had carried in my pocket. We had arrived in Paradise—the olive trees, the stone house next to the creek, the grape vines, looked exactly like those in Neapoli, where we had begun. Why had we made the effort to hike here? The only difference from where we had started was the perspective. At a higher elevation, we enjoyed a more expansive view.

In a flash, I understood: Paradise is not an ultimate destination. There is nothing in Paradise that we do not already have; there is nothing to look forward to. Paradise is wherever we find ourselves, here and now, today.

Theia Chrysoula's Shoes

ALEXA TSAKOPOULOS

꙳

I had to give Theia Chrysoula her shoes. I buried the simple, black flats wrapped in tissue paper under a pile of carelessly folded shirts in my suitcase, tucking the sleeves of a white polo shirt around them to ensure a safe trip. My mother had given me the shoes to hand-deliver to my cherished *thiea* (aunt). Theia Chrysoula was the first cousin of my grandmother. She had held me on her lap when I was two years old, the first time my eyes grasped the beautiful land of my family.

As a little girl, I used to stare into her deep-set, almond eyes in wonder. How does the unforgiving summer sun fail to convince her to remove her heavy, black dress? I didn't know it was a dress of mourning, the darkness signifying respect for the husband that she had lost, and bringing some solace to her aching heart. From her dress, my eyes danced back to her face, round and kind. Her hair was gathered in a tight knot at the nape of her neck, the thin strands surrendering to the command of her headscarf. Her face was like a fresco I had seen in a church. Once rich in color and vitality, time had drawn a labyrinth of cracks and lines, and dampened its hues. Moving to her mouth, my eyes traced the lines of her lips. Although I could barely understand her words, since I could not speak Greek well, the sweet, strong sounds rooted me to my Greek ancestry.

"*Alexoula moo, s'agapo* (my Alexa, I love you)," she whispered.

"*Ke ego s'agapo* (And I love you)" I replied.

Abruptly waking up to the sound of *Ice Ice Baby* ringing my cellular phone, I rolled over, pulling the covers over my head. We were leaving Sacramento that afternoon, and the dread of abandoning my friends had been plaguing me. I was not ready to leave for Greece. I had spent the first month of my summer holiday in pleasurable pursuits with my two best girlfriends. We lounged by the pool by day and drove around Sacramento by night, blasting the *macarena* and dancing. We went to the amusement park, watched funny movies, and duplicated craft projects we had seen on the Home and Garden channel. I was not yet ready to be plucked from home, and thrown into the loneliness of travel. I did not want to give up my California summer lifestyle.

It wasn't that I didn't love Greece. I loved letting my eyes skip from row to row of olive trees as we drove down to Vatika, my eyes settling on the straight path for a moment, before the next line of trees rushed past. I delighted in seeing ruins of temples and shrines sprinkled among modern buildings, a fusion of past and present. I especially treasured sitting at a taverna with my family, shaded from the incandescent summer sun, playfully arguing over who got to eat the last *kolokithokeftede* (zucchini fritter). I loved the warm glow that infused my time in Greece, but I was not ready to trade the *macarena* for a *zeimbekiko*, or the amusement park for any ancient ruins.

Maybe it was because I never really felt comfortable speaking Greek. I was not ready to sacrifice myself again at the altar of mistaken verbal conjugations and improper noun-adjective agreement. I was hesitant to don the scarlet "alpha" which in this case stood for "aaaah . . . " the sound I used to deflect attention from the fact that I could not put together a proper sentence in the short time allotted before the next person would chime into the conversation. I was not ready to be forced into fumbling silence.

Even though almost everyone in Neapoli spoke English, they felt compelled to speak to me in Greek. It was, after all, my heritage. Somehow that pressure always made it so much more difficult to ask which way to the local taverna. It was only with Theia Chrysoula that I was able to communicate fearlessly. As I walked to her house, past the green trash bins, I spotted the scattered steppingstones from the corner, recognizing the aged terracotta squares and the weeds that snaked in between them. Hopping from square to square with my feet joined as one, I passed pots filled with roses, four o'clocks, marigolds, and rose-scented geraniums. I ducked under the arbor, avoiding bunches of grapes, and looked up at patches of sky that peeked through the twisted vines. Lost in the puzzle pieces of light blue, my attention was diverted by a tiny, wooden gate. Peering over the top, I saw a vegetable garden filled with fresh, ripe produce. The tomatoes hung inside the confines of a gated barrel, and the scent of chamomile delighted me. It was as abundant as I remembered, bearing fruits, vegetables and herbs for our mid-afternoon lunches. I left the garden and made my way inside the house. Climbing the five steps that led to the screen door, I was startled when it swung open ahead of me. Theia Chrysoula smiled at me, her almond eyes luminous. She reached out her arms and hugged me. I felt the warmth of her embrace.

Theia Chrysoula took my arm in hers, leading me through the screen door, through the tiny kitchen, and into the living room. Sitting on her maroon, floral print couch, she asked me about the family and all the new gossip. It was there, in the home of my aunt that I was able to speak unreservedly. I chatted away, not worried about my broken Greek, humiliation forgotten. Remembering the reason I had come, I reached for the gift I had brought with me. I smiled and gently passed the tightly wrapped shoes to my aunt. She carefully parted the tissue paper to reveal the shoes. A little-girl smile illuminated her face and she clapped her hands together with delight, as if it was the first pair of shoes she had ever received. She excitedly leaned over and embraced me yet again.

"*Alexoula mou, s'agapo,*" she whispered to me.

"*Ke ego s'agapo,*" I replied.

As she eagerly raised the right shoe out of the box, I looked at it carefully. It was a black, flat shoe with two crisscrossed straps over the toes. Although the shoes were cute, I probably wouldn't wear them. I'd opt for a more chic, embellished shoe, something with more character. My journey to bring Theia Chrysoula shoes seemed like a twist of the Cinderella fairytale: I was bringing her the acclaimed slipper. I left her house in high spirits, glad that I had delivered the shoes and done as I was asked. And I left with something more: a feeling of family unity, belonging, and love.

Back in California, I walked across the white marble floor of Nordstrom department store. The air conditioner was blowing and a piano played softly in the background. My friends and I excitedly browsed the first floor shoe department. "Ooh, those Steve Madden pumps are pretty cute," my friend cooed. I had been back for three days, back into my California lifestyle just in time for the end of summer. As my friends and I wove through the stands of shoes, our eyes darted from wedges to sneakers. "Flats are really in now, and they're comfortable, too," my other friend chimed in. As we approached the stand of fashionable flats, I spotted the shoes that had brought so much joy to my dear aunt. I decided to try them on. They *were* comfortable and stylish. They were plain, but they reminded me of the way Theia Chrysoula smiled when she first saw them. They were perfect.

What My Father Dreams

"*The sleep of the dead is so deep that all who walk it dream . . .* "
—HENRY MILLER, *THE COLOSSUS OF MAROUSSI*

I have come here, Father,
your new ashes still unscattered,
to seek the way of the living.
Yet in every sleep I find your face,
your dream.

You traveled once to this honeyed land
and brought me a golden necklace,
finely woven as Athena's hair.
I came after, and brought you
as my gift

a holy icon in three parts,
saintly faces edged with gold.
Unfolded, it sat on your desk
shining with that light from
another world.

Now I have returned
and the light of all Greece shines
on your face—your photo, my icon –
as if ready to speak.
But what are you dreaming now?

That although this land is not
our land, still I might find you
here, in this place where
the living and the dead are
not afraid to meet?

That although these seas are not
our seas, when I swim in waters
clear as the color of God's blue eye,
I feel you there, too,
swimming along with me?

Or that under every living rock
upended, there is a story you forgot to tell
whispered through the oleanders and palms,
like the ones on the street in California
where you were born?

Or perhaps when I sail,
not as a warrior like you,
but as a seeker, crossing
the secrets of the sunken city,
lost in that Lakonian Sea,

I will find among its shimmering towers
and golden fishes, its treasures,
gone but to the realm of imagining,
your spirit,
alive and speaking

from that watery womb.
There, where past and present flow together,
and gods and angels spin
the silken threads of
mortals' lives

there, Father, I can walk deep with you,
hear your voice,
your dreams,
and sleep again
the bearable sleep of the living.

—JOANNA BIGGAR

Topless on Elafonisos

ANNE WOODS

꙳

I have always wanted to swim topless. There were many reasons why I had not. Shyness and modesty, and fear of being arrested for indecent exposure were at the top of my list, as was fear of being leered at. When we arrived at Simos beach and Virginia and Connie, our Greek workshop hosts, discarded their bikini tops, I knew this might be my chance. Other women were swimming, sunbathing, and strolling casually up and down the beach with their bosoms warming in the midday sun.

I had been tempted to swim topless several times before, once in Hawaii, when I was the only person on the beach. Something held me back though. It was like arriving at the edge of the high dive and looking over to realize just how far down the water is.

This past April I felt that defeat again as I watched the Kohala coast of Hawaii's Big Island recede away through the window of an Aloha Airlines 737. Puako Reef glistened below, white coral and veins of black lava clearly visible through the crystalline water. Would I ever muster the courage to swim topless? When would we be back? A year maybe? Little did I know that in four months I would be standing on that precipice of possibility once again, opportunity open before me like the whole ocean.

My desire was not for exhibition. Water, beaches, and seashells have been obsessions of mine for as long as I can remember. I have a large collection of the latter. All of them I have gathered myself. Even if they are fragments, as many of the shells are, they are still beautiful to me. They are symbols for me, potent as a scent, that can recall a place. Collecting them allows me to purge all thoughts from my mind and focus on the moment. The lull of waves and the feel of sand on my bare feet intoxicate me. And water: the first thing I want to do when I arrive at a place near it is to get in. I am not a scuba diver, nor am I fond of extreme water sports. The act of floating, buoyant in salt water, of looking back at the shore in awe of the earth, centers me. It strips away years of conditioning. It allows me to reconnect with my own position in the world. In these moments I am not wife, daughter, sister, or friend. I am a woman.

The sand on Simos beach, on the island of Elafonisos, is fine and white like the dusting of powdered sugar on a Mexican wedding cookie. It is composed of minerals from eroded rocks, as is the sand in California. Millions of years of geology slid between my toes as I walked on it. The sandy bottom makes a long and shallow retreat through light blue water, receding away into darker and darker shades of ocean. The beach is nearly half-moon shaped. It is sheltered by a small hill on its north edge that forms the barrier between Simos beach and Megali Paralia beach. The waves were gentle. They were not the crashing waves of Hawaii, with their throaty howl as they grind over a shallow reef, tossing up bits of cowry shells and rust and white coral. Dunes surround Simos beach. They are dotted with clumps of tall grasses, the color of finely ground coriander.

But it was the water that drew me. It was not the deep blue of a blueberry, or lapis lazuli, or ink. Nor was it the bright, bright blue of the Greek islands that is fluorescent against whitewashed houses. It was a cerulean blue: blue like the sky, but not the sky alone. There was aquamarine that was icy clear. Clear, clear, clear like a glass of cold water on a hot day. It quenched the thirst of my eyes. It was an aqueous mix of blues and greens, the color of my husband's eyes.

"The water is so clear you want to drink it," a taxi driver in Athens said to me when I told him I had been to Simos beach. Elafonisos' bright white sand, clean water and shallow depths create this mesmerizing aqua color. It is what I remember about water. It is how I catalog places in my mind. Elafonisos reminded me of the eastern shores of Baja, Mexico, those long stretches of ivory beaches that bleed into the electric blues of the Gulf of Mexico. Even the landscape, mostly barren of trees, reminded me of Baja, though the midpoint of the Baja Peninsula lies nine degrees closer to the equator.

The island of Elafonisos is a twenty-minute ferry ride across the bay from Neapoli, Vatika's largest town. It sits in the Gulf of Lakonia, on the southern Ionian Sea. The twelve-square-mile island has been inhabited since Neolithic times, and the first settlement in Vatika is believed to have been on Elafonisos. It is a relatively young island. The narrow isthmus that connected it to the Peloponnese mainland was severed in 375 A.D., when an earthquake struck.

Simos beach is on the island's western side, surrounded by the Bay of Frangou. The name, *Frangou*, rolls off my tongue like melting chocolate when I say it. Its decadent sound does justice to the beauty of its water.

"You have to swim!" our host Connie, called out incredulously to Catherine.

"No. I really don't want to swim," Catherine replied. "I didn't even bring my bathing suit."

"Swim in your underwear. Nobody will care," Connie urged.

"Oh, but I don't want to get my underwear wet," Catherine said, hoping to strike a deal.

Barbara held up a pair of white and orange striped panties and a white cotton tee-shirt. "You can wear these," she said, "so you don't get yours wet."

"But I really want to use this time to get some writing done," Catherine said. She didn't stand a chance. Part of me felt sorry for her. She had made a plan to relax and to write, under the shade of a beach umbrella. I couldn't imagine a more soothing place to write. But, the other part of me knew she would regret not getting into the water.

"Catherine," I said, "if you go in, I'll go topless." I said it quickly, before my brain caught up with my mouth. Now I was committed. But how would I do it? Would I wade into the sea and remove my bikini top under cover of water? Or would I do it as I was walking away from everyone, and then quickly submerge myself? No, I decided. I would do this gracefully, like a Greek woman.

Catherine was still resisting as a tent of multi-colored towels was erected around her. Barbara handed her the panties and tee-shirt.

Doreen, also without a bathing suit, was similarly persuaded to strip to her underwear. Doreen is always well-dressed. Some of us just put on whatever is clean; Doreen wears outfits. Her clothes not only match themselves, but they compliment her hair, her skin tone, her jewelry. So, when I saw her walking elegantly across the sand in her matching skin-tone bra and panties, breasts held high, I was not surprised. Of course Doreen's underclothes matched.

Catherine emerged from the makeshift towel cabana and headed for the water, stylish and graceful, even in borrowed clothes. It was my turn. I reached behind my neck and untied the knot holding my brown-and-white-flower-print bikini top around my shoulders. I unhooked the back clasp and threw the top on the chaise lounge. If I do it too slowly, I told myself, I may change my mind.

I ran across the hot sand and felt relief as my toes hit the cool water. As soon as I was fully submerged I realized I had forgotten something important. Sunscreen. It was alright when I was trotting away from everybody, but now I was going to have to walk toward them, to retrieve the pale green tube of SPF 30 sunscreen sitting next to my abandoned bikini top. What the heck, I said to myself as

I walked back toward the sunbathers. I slathered the lotion on what was soon-to-be-formerly-lily-white skin and returned to the water.

The water felt like a lukewarm bath. The shallow depths and closely orbiting July sun had warmed the Bay of Frangou. The heat I felt from having made the three-quarter-mile trek across the virtually treeless island from where the ferry had dropped us off melted away when my body hit the water.

It started at my feet. The sting of hot sand on their bare, pink undersides made the sudden submersion in the water sweeter, like walking across uneven pebbles, and then deeply-piled velvet. It was the kind of transition that is instantaneous, but leaves you recounting it in your mind afterward, over and over. You are reluctant to let go, even though you know more is coming.

Two round and friendly-looking Greek men, appearing to be in their mid-sixties, swam over to me. "Where are you from?" one asked in heavily-accented, but flawless English.

"San Francisco," I said.

"We used to own a Greek restaurant in San Francisco," the other replied. The wife of the first man joined us. Her golden skin was weathered by the sun like a well-used leather purse, still appearing soft, but worn. Her lips were lacquered bright red, outlined with pencil and filled in with lipstick. Her face was spackled with foundation. Eyelashes black as midnight. Bosoms overflowing from the top of a metallic orange one piece.

"Where are you going after here?" she asked, smiling broadly.

"I am not sure," I said. "Maybe Santorini. Where would you recommend?"

Her hands popped out of the water before her mouth opened. "Oh, you have to go to Mykonos! You must!" She gesticulated wildly, her arms and hands circling about her head like a medusa's snakes. "Go to Super Paradise beach when you get there. It's amazing!"

"You even talked to those men topless," Catherine said after I swam to where she was bobbing in the water. I had forgotten for a few minutes that I was topless. Though I did not go there, I would later learn that Super Paradise beach caters to partying and frequently nude Europeans.

Aphrodite, goddess of love and beauty, is said to have risen from the foam of the sea near the island of Kythira, just four miles south of Elafonisos. I imagined this as I floated in the waters of her birth. The water felt like a gown, ruffles of silk brushing against my body as I moved. "It is better, isn't it? Swimming without a top," Virginia asked as we passed one another in the water.

"Yes, it's amazing," I replied. It was better than I had imagined.

"How do you say *joie de vivre* in Greek?"

"*Chara tis zois,*" Virginia replied.

"What then shall we choose? Weight or lightness?" wrote Milan Kundera in *The Unbearable Lightness of Being*. It is a purposeful decision to choose lightness, for we are deluged with weight by the nature of our consciousness.

The air smelled fresh and clean, not salty like a beach with waves. I inhaled. The sun warmed me. I was free as I floated. I plucked courage from the edge of the sea. It was sweet surrender. It was a perfect moment.

Matters of the Heart:
Discovering Dionysus

DOREEN WOOD

)

I was once on a cruise in the Greek Islands with two hundred psychiatrists. My husband, Don, a professor of transportation, and I had been in Sweden for two months on a teaching assignment and were completing the European visit with a trip to more southern climes.

Don and I had been on the ship for scarcely an hour when we talked with a pleasant middle-aged man. He told us that he was a psychiatrist. At the late night buffet, our table mates were another psychiatrist and her literature professor husband.

"That's funny," I said, "We keep meeting psychiatrists on this ship. Are you all doing therapy or what?"

"Oh, no," our dinner companion responded coolly. "We're here for study. Once a year we have to do continuing education to keep our licenses. We have to go to lectures every day."

"Wow," I said. "A Greek cruise and psychiatric education. What a great way to get a tax deduction!" I have graduate degrees in behavioral disabilities; I wished I'd known about this kind of educational cruise years ago.

Another therapist invited me to sit in on a presentation on modern treatment modalities for an Oedipus complex. In the dimmed light of the lecture hall, a doctor presented his findings on what had or hadn't worked for patients.

"Thirty-four percent of the study group responded well to a combination of group and individual therapy," he said. He flipped to another slide on his circular projector.

"Now, here are the data for patients who had no intervention."

One doctor raised his hand, as serious faces scribbled into their notebooks. "It looks as if you don't know what happens with this group."

"I have no answers," the lecturer replied.

"Huh?" I thought. "They've been studying the psyche for years, and they have no answers?" This was the thing that troubled me most in my years as a medical professional. It always seemed like empirical data was the only information that mattered to most of my colleagues. I'd often felt that many physicians stay a protective step removed from the pain and suffering of their patients. What about humanity and heart? What about intuition?

The days went by. We cruised. We toured the ruins. Ancient Greek history and mythology haunted my thoughts. The Greeks seemed so wise in their integration of mind, body, and spirit. But what about me, my husband, the academics with whom we inter-acted, the psychiatrists on this ship? Where was the connection between all this intellectualism and healing of the mind?

There were no psychiatrists on my next trip to Greece, five years later, nor was I traveling with my husband. I had lost Don two years earlier. I was now alone and had decided to return to Greece, this time to attend a writing workshop. I was in Vatika on the southern tip of the Peloponnese, high in the village of Mesochori.

Five hours by van had brought eleven writers to a ten-day workshop in this beautiful, remote area. When we arrived, our co-ordinator, Connie, an expatriate and local resident, leapt into the van with a warm yell of greeting. Dark curls flying, her eyes spar-kling and her arms outspread, she planted a kiss, first in the middle of one cheek, then the other, of each and every one of us. My surprised cheeks remained cool as her plum-like lips pressed into them. Unaccustomed to such a flood of hospitality and energy, I tried not to flinch.

The dirt road leading to our hostess Virginia's home was so narrow that our van had to stop on a promontory about sixty feet above her house. We waited for her to ascend and greet us. Leaping out of her little car, clad in a white toga, she also planted a delicate kiss on the cheeks of each and every one.

In the following days, I witnessed this expressive form of greet-ing everywhere. Down at the beachfront in the small port town of Neapoli one day, I saw Connie spot a friend. She embraced the woman and kissed her twice. The two loudly chattered on in Greek.

Taxis picked us up every day to wildly transport us on excursions. We'd already met our Canadian neighbors, John and Mary, who live in Mesochori for six months of the year. On one of these rendezvous with our Greek drivers, John was standing nearby. Our driver leapt out of his cab, darted over to John and they threw their arms around each other and kissed each other on each cheek. Another volley of Greek exclamations followed.

I imagined that many of the people I was meeting, like me, had been close to illness, deaths, and divorces. Surely their losses had been as devastating as mine. But I was also seeing that these people continued to sing, cry, shout, and act with generosity and kindness. Was this for real? I'd worn a fairly impermeable shell for much of my life. My husband's world, the one in which I'd circulated, was one of detachment and cool civility. I had long yearned to break free, to act with abandonment and ecstasy, to connect with life.

On the fourth day of our stay, our group traveled on Captain Vassilis' *caique* to the craggy island of Elafonisos. As we clutched supports against the strength of the bumping waves, he handed the boat controls over to his son, and walked into our midst. Captain Vassilis put his arm around Virginia's shoulder and for the rest of the twenty-five-minute boat ride, with his face flushed, his eyes melting, the two of them sang lyrical Greek melodies.

"*S'agapo, s'agapo,*
S'agapo yiati ise oraia"

130

I love you, I love you,
I love you because you are beautiful.

I was transported into the reality of song, white-capped waves and whistling *meltemi* winds.

The boat docked and we clambered out and picked our way along the stony path to Simos beach. I was unaware that I was about to strip. Reaching the beach, I reveled in the creamy soft sand, as soft as a bed of icing sugar segueing into the changing blues and greens of the Aegean Sea. My plan was to quietly ensconce myself on a beach chair with my book and the nearby comfort of my companions. I had no bathing suit in my bag. But a voice from the water called out, "Come in, Doreen, come in. Come on. Take off your top and shorts."

I hesitated, then replied, "Okay, okay. Why not?"

Exposed, I stood, my nearly bared breasts held high. The sun warmed my slim body as I put my feet into the caressing water, water so clear that I could see tiny fish darting around my legs and little black crabs keeping me company on the bottom. Confidence rising, I ventured further out. Breathing, breathing deeply into my belly, I bent my knees and plunged into the sea, a shock of pleasure coursing through me. My body rolled, writhed beneath the surface until I was ready to climb back up onto the silky sand.

Men and women of varied shapes clustered the beach. As is the custom in this part of the world, many of the women were topless. Some were fat and droopy, others scrawny and flat. No one gave any notice. But I thought I was hearing things when to my delight, a voice beside me said, "You have a very nice body!"

What a personal comment to hear from a stranger. But somehow, in this context, it was O.K. . . . more than O.K.—it was great.

Several hours later and still on the island, we all went to eat at a taverna. The wooden tables and chairs, covered with blue and white plastic, were outside under a tarpaulin, and directly across a walkway where fishermen's boats were tied to the docks. The owner proudly showed his catch of the day, a fat fish resembling a red snapper. It tantalized our taste buds when it was presented to us on a large platter, baked to perfection with a lemon-olive oil glaze. Jugs of wine and baskets of crusty bread sat on the table. We ate bowls of deliciously seasoned green beans, fried zucchini blossoms and freshly steamed beets. We consumed plentiful bowls of Greek salad with fresh slabs of creamy feta cheese, arugula, ruby-red tomatoes, sliced onions, cucumbers and Kalamata olives, all simply dressed with olive oil and salt.

Townspeople clustered around us as Virginia and Captain Vassilis renewed their singing. One young man, his tawny hair pulled back into a ponytail, flashing the whitest teeth imaginable, wandered over to our table.

"Doctor Pericles, Doctor Pericles!" exclaimed Captain Vassilis. "Welcome! Sit down!"

I was drawn to him. This easygoing young man was unlike any doctor I'd met. He did not exhibit the detachment of physicians I had known—including those I encountered as my husband was dying.

His wide smile warmed my heart when I heard him say, "I know I've helped people even though I was quite scared when I arrived on Elafonisos seven months ago. At first I was calling the big city clinics for advice, but now find that I don't need to do that as much. These villagers are set in their ways and keep their sick people inside their houses. They think that they will get better faster if they take double the amount of their prescriptions, so I have to dole out their prescriptions a dose at a time."

I imagined him in his clinic down the alley, wearing his crisp white jacket, waiting for his patients. I could see him checking his stock of medications and lining up his instruments.

He stopped talking to us to kiss two young children who came running up to meet him.

"Both of them had the most terrible chest infections this winter. Look at them now. And see that man over there, the one pulling in his nets from his boat? A few months ago he was gasping for breath, and I was able to help him find the right heart medication. Now he sings in the taverna every night."

Doctor Pericles went on to say that his first university studies in Athens were in fine arts and that he sees his work in medicine as a synthesis of these two disciplines. Practicing medicine is also a form of art.

"Aha!" I thought to myself. "Doctor Pericles has brought it together!"

The Greeks say that there are two parts to the consciousness. The culture of the ancient Greeks encompassed the intuitive world of Dionysus and the intellectual world of Apollo. The god Dionysus represents intuition, excitement with life and all of our senses. Song and dance and theatre were included in his realm. To this day, worshippers of Dionysus must have enthusiasm—the god within themselves. They strive to achieve ecstasy, to move outside of themselves and embrace the world.

On the other hand, the sun god Apollo represents an analytical, brilliant intellectualism. Much of our modern day culture of empirical data and reasoning is closer to the Apollonian mindset, and in our modern society, we've become separated from our Dionysian intuition. I was beginning to see that to truly connect with life—to dance, to sing, to feel—is a great gift to oneself.

The original Greek concept of the word, *psyche*, includes the modern ideas of soul, self and mind. In modern day Greece, expressiveness in matters of the heart is the norm. I had learned something that I could never have found on that Greek cruise so many years ago, the one populated by psychiatrists. I had found my way back to my emotions, to a moment when a greeting, a kindness and a kiss can dispel the darkness that the death of a loved one—in this case, my beloved Don—can produce. I had found, what the Greeks have known all along—that the heart is the true root of the psyche.

Swimming with Cyclops

Joanna Biggar

꒜

On a brief taxi ride through Athens, the driver took it upon himself to play tour guide as well, pointing out the sights as I sped past. Waving at some impressive columns, he shouted, "That is the temple of Zeus." It did look majestic, but, well . . . lonely. That got me to thinking: 'What ever happened to old Zeus anyway? In fact, where do any of the old gods go when the new team comes in?'

I puzzled over this for days as I traveled from Athens to the region of Vatika in the southern Peloponnese. The landscape of Greece is littered with the temples, statues, and lore of the gods who are so past their prime, so last millennium—O.K. last three millennia. Then it came to me in a flash while swimming at one of Greece's most glorious beaches: I couldn't say where they had been hiding out all these years, but rather than being voted off the island, they were right there *on* the island, summering in Elafonisos, swimming and sunning along with me!

The revelation came to me like this: In the horseshoe-shaped bay at Simos beach, I was aware—mindful is perhaps the word—that this island was the reputed home of a Cyclops, the one-eyed giant who terrified Odysseus—and ate some of his crew—as he sailed these seas on his long voyage home. As I swam further out in the clear water of many blues, I couldn't help wondering, *was a monstrous Cyclops still slumbering in a nearby cave?* Then I saw him, a huge hirsute creature with wild grey hair. As he lowered himself from a yacht anchored near the mouth of the bay into a zodiac, he pulled on a facemask and soon dove into the water not far from me. There he was, a one-eyed monster swimming right past me! It all became too clear when the zodiac, steered by a fellow creature from the yacht, neared shore. Cyclops jumped on just in time to grab some unsuspecting tourists in large hats onto the boat with him. In no time, they were all back climbing the ladder to the yacht, and I wondered at the fate of his passengers. Lunch, perhaps?

After that near-miss, I pulled myself up on the beach to re-cover and to digest what I had just experienced, and wondered if anyone else had witnessed what I had. As I glanced tentatively around, a near neighbor on a beach cot under an umbrella caught my eye. Zeus! There he was clear as day, though now with an impressive post-middle-aged belly. Perhaps he was out of practice throwing his thunderbolt. But from the looks of it, even though he hadn't been too visible these several centuries, he still seemed to be running the world right there from the beach on his cell phone. It appeared to be permanently affixed to the hand against his ear, leaving only one hand free to make sweeping, god-like CEO gestures. Remembering how forlorn his abandoned temple in Athens had looked, I realized he was still on top on his game and savvy enough to remain Master of the Universe. A Greek cross hung on a chain upon his hairy chest.

And there next to him, wonder of wonders, was Hera, the long-suffering sister, wife, take your pick. One thing about Zeus: When it came to the ladies, he was highly indiscriminate. That of course, had been Hera's beef all along, and her revenge for his dalliances had been the stuff of gossip rags for the ages. But after all this time, they'd hung in there, and she was beside him still—though he'd hogged the shade and she was turning lobster red in too much sun. Obviously she needed a new sun cream, and the many-colored straw hat wasn't doing much for her either. But she seemed content enough, nose buried in a movie magazine.

Stunned at this revelation, I sat up and my eye swept the beach. The gods, the heroes, the mortals they toyed with, they were all there! There was Cupid looking not a day over thirty-five, with only a slight bulge above his Speedo, strutting along beside a very tanned and fit Psyche, who no doubt kept her figure after childbirth by putting hours in at the Olympian Gym. Their three offspring toddled after them eating ice cream, the youngest the spitting image of his father, a cherub with a pacifier trailing a bow and arrow.

Persephone was in front of them, stunning too in her topless bikini and newly streaked hair, stepping out of the sea. Clearly it was she, as her jealous husband, who would hardly let her more than three feet away, glowered after her. A gossip sheet left on the beach informed me that she'd done well this season with her own line of perfumes on a Spring theme, and that next she was going into designer beachwear named "Hotter than Hades."

No such luck though, for a once-petite ex-beauty queen bulging out of her tent-like suit further down the beach. Though attempting to hide under a beach towel and behind Jackie-O-sized shades, unquestionably it was Helen of Troy, a three hundred-pounder with wrinkles and a bad dye job! It was heartbreaking to see what could happen to a girl who let herself go for three thousand years. The gossip sheet noted that although she'd been under wraps for a long time, she was soon checking into a French health spa for a complete makeover. I had to hope so. It was too sad, really, to notice that all her possessions were tucked in a well-worn shopping bag embossed with the words *City of Paris.*

A red-faced fellow with a well-trimmed white beard was also coming out of the water, where he had been playing with a rubber trident. Without question, it was Poseidon, who evidently was taking the summer off from his world-wide storm-making franchise, which had become so successful that of late it's a key player in all global markets, to say nothing of global realignments. For the season he was running a ferry to the mainland, and I overheard someone say one of the favored destinations was the Vatistas Winery in Neapoli, where Dionysus served as chief winemaker-in-residence, pushing the best regional wines.

Even Socrates made the scene, long white hair flowing around that devilishly satyr-like face, not looking any different, best I could tell, from when he made his supposedly final appearance, following that unfortunate cocktail chugging incident in 399 B.C. I was surprised, I admit, to see his particular comeback, but maybe that's what was meant by being an immortal of philosophy. Anyway, he was clearly intent on swimming far out into dangerous currents, and was obviously headed for Cyclops's yacht which had receded further into the sea. I overheard someone say that he just wanted "to dialogue" with the monster.

I decided to walk along the shore to take in what I was experiencing, but was nearly knocked down by a well-oiled, hugely muscled brute leading a pack of youths jogging down the sand, exercising their Achilles tendons. Heracles, I thought. Or perhaps not—maybe the Governor of California. Gods, heroes, stuntmen, movie stars . . . it was getting hard to tell. That fact was driven home a minute later when I spied a gaggle of bronzed, muscular young men with gold chains around their necks staring with concentration toward the sea. Ah, I thought, well-preserved veterans of the Trojan War recovering on the beach. But alas, as I got closer, I realized they were just Italian tourists, doing what they do best, checking out the local nymphs.

At that precise moment, there was the abrupt roaring of an engine, and all eyes turned toward the sand dunes as they parted to unleash a shiny Harley Davidson and its rider, a shirtless young man in tight jeans, with six-pack abs and a fashionable two days' growth of stubble. The previously mellow crowd was instantly energized by his arrival; a concerted cheer rose up, followed by undercurrents of murmuring. *At last,* they mumbled, *about time, late again.* 'Who *is* this dude?' I had to ask myself. But then I saw the stylish leather bag slung across one shoulder. It sported the name *Hermes.* Of course, the messenger. As the crowd got more agitated, I wondered if he was on the verge of being shot for bringing the message. Or for not bringing it.

Closed down the ouzo bar in port again, I heard. *Stumbling around at dawn (well, 10:30 a.m.) looking for a good Greek coffee. Missed his morning rendezvous, missed the photo op. Where in Hades IS she?*

It took me awhile to piece together the story, but everyone calmed down when he pulled out a paper from his bag and read what could only be called a press release. It seemed that even the gods had their idols, and all had been waiting for The Event of the season, the arrival of the super-goddess, Aphrodite, who looked— according to her press agent—as dewy, fresh and irresistible as she had the day she first stepped out of the sea in a swirl of foam. That event, as everyone knew, had taken place not far away, just off the neighboring island of Kythira, visible offshore.

"She's been revisiting her home waters," Hermes shouted to all, "but will be making her arrival tomorrow at ten. A chartered yacht has been arranged."

I had to worry that Cyclops might be involved, but the crowd seemed generally appeased. Hermes, his message delivered, silently pushed his bike back over the dunes, forgotten and, evidently, forgiven.

But my mind was a swirl, and I went back to my beach chair to recoup. It was astonishing really how these gods could come and go, could reinvent themselves in whatever forms they liked. I was still uncertain where exactly they had been all these centuries, or where they would show up next season, but it was clear to me that their hiding places were closer at hand then your basic human might think. I began to imagine what the dawn would bring, with Aphrodite's coming and all. The other beachgoers certainly had no doubts about her arrival, about her appearance, about the *affect* of her grand entrance.

But I began to wonder: How could they be sure? With the gods' abilities at transformation, how could they tell she wasn't among them already, in some kind of earthly disguise. She might, for example, be hiding out as some mere mortal. A foreigner, maybe, of undistinguishable age wearing a nondescript black bathing suit. She might be that very woman under the big sun hat—who was looking unexpectedly good, you'd have to admit. Yes, why not? The one scribbling in her notebook, taking it all down. . . .

Matiasmeni

CONNIE BURKE

>–

An icon of the Holy Lady hung above the nightstand, calm
and compassionate, absorbing the silent screams, the voice
of pain echoing in the darkness of the hour. Areti's eyes blinked
rapidly, scanning the room, as the throbbing in her head became
more intense. Her fists clenched against her stiffened hip joints.
Waves of pain shuddered through her young body, as an all too
familiar queasiness mounted, like Etna rising, from the gut of
her stomach. Grimacing, I looked away as she vomited into the
dented tin bowl her grandmother had placed on the floor next
to the white, wrought-iron bed. Areti was desperate, calling the

Pleiades to her bedside, begging the Holy Lady for mercy, imploring her seventy-two-year-old yiayia for help.

I helped Areti's yiayia (grandmother) drape a thick red tablecloth over the closed wooden shutters to block out the thin rays of light that slanted into this dark, silent space. Yiayia's gnarled hands quickly cut up thin strips of white muslin cloth. She handed them to me. One strip at a time, I dipped the cloth into a ceramic bowl of cold spring water, wrung it out and placed it tenderly on Areti's forehead. The coolness of the cloth brought little comfort. Pain pulsated through her body like venom. We could do nothing. Areti was suffering from what seemed like a terrible migraine.

"What triggered it this time?" I wondered. "Was it the sweltering heat of summer, the bright light of the midday August sun, a chemical reaction to food or alcohol, her period? Or was it the *Mati*, the legendary Evil Eye?"

The Greek Orthodox Church calls the Evil Eye *Vaskania*, a derivative of the Latin word *fascinato*. No Greek argues whether it exists or not. It simply does. In Vatika, it is popularly called the *Mati*. Superstitions surrounding the *Mati* exist throughout the world, especially in the Mediterranean countries, Mexico, and Central America. The ancient Greeks believed that some malignant influence darted from the eyes of envious or angry persons and infected the air with a pernicious quality that could penetrate and corrupt the bodies of living creatures and inanimate objects. Even flowers and trees have been affected.

Yet, I was surprised to learn that inflicting the *Mati* is usually involuntary. Perpetrators do not intend to use it, and are usually not aware they are doing so. No wrongdoing or revenge is sought against another person. The perpetrators are victims themselves, but victims who escape the malignity by passing it on, as if by reflex. They are usually envious people, those who continually praise children or gaze at them without touching them, those who suffer from covetousness, or childless women.

According to Greek lore, almost anything could indicate that some person suffered from the *Mati*. If a child got sick, some possession was lost or stolen, animals died, or crops failed, one suspected the *Mati*. People with blue eyes or men with bushy eyebrows could inflict the Mati. Groucho?

Undoubtedly "people watching" is the most popular pastime throughout the villages of Vatika. It is no surprise that the belief in the *Mati* is popular here. The local *cafenions* are packed with men and women observing and discussing passersby. Just watching, one might project envy for another's fashionable attire, education, wealth, a healthy look, or a beautiful face, thus giving them the Evil Eye.

Areti has a beautiful face. At twenty-two, she stands tall, like a caryatid overlooking a great city, proud and serene. Her skin is tanned by an early summer sun; her light brown hair, the length of a wave, caresses the shores of her shoulders. Her long narrow hands could hold nothing but flowers.

When Areti became ill, her yiayia told me she was *matiasmeni*—that she suffered from the Evil Eye, *Mati*. Affected individuals can experience fatigue, headaches, or other kinds of physical pain. They can experience paralysis in their arms and legs, dizziness, nausea, tremors, and a heavy sweat. Their eyes blur, they mumble, and experience spasms.

"If a person receives the evil eye while walking, they can fall to the ground shaking and afraid," her yiayia murmured as she pulled back the faded black scarf that covered her sparse gray hair. "Their ears buzz and their stomachs ache," she added. "They also experience severe depression."

Later on I found out that even animals may fall to the ground and moan with pain. They will stop eating and when pulled, will not stand up. Sheep that have received the *Mati* while giving birth will be unable to nurse their lambs.

Areti's *Mati* brought about a debilitating migraine. Pain pills, beta blockers, or acetaminophen could not relieve it. She did not dare look at the marigolds, verbena, and portulaca growing through soft tussocks of grass beneath the trees that lined the footpath outside her grandmother's door. Light and color were vexing. The furies were with her, whistling in the room as the old floorboards creaked with every footstep. Areti lay motionless. She was waiting for Kyria Kaneli (Mrs. Kaneli), the *ksematiastra*, the spell-breaker from the nearby town of Kambos, west of Neapoli.

"Kyria Kaneli knows what to do," her yiayia sighed. "She will be cured," she added with conviction.

Cures against the Evil Eye's curses are as ancient and numerous as the curses themselves. In Vatika, the techniques of *ksematiasma* (spell-breaking) are handed down orally from man to woman and vice versa. But in Vatika, the *ksematiastra* is always a woman. The association of the *Mati* with women, be it as victim or spell-breaker, may arise from the tendency of women to be more sensitive to body language than men, and therefore hold on to certain "magic." If I wanted to learn the incantations that would help remove the *Mati*, I would have to learn them from a man. If my sister wanted to learn them, I would have to teach them to a man, who, in turn, could teach them to my sister. This system is as ancient as the land itself.

When Kyria Kaneli arrived, she wasted no time. She understood the symptoms and immediately recognized the effects of a serious *Mati*. At first, she put a few drops of olive oil into a bowl of salted water. If the oil scattered, forming blobs, Areti would not be seriously *Matiasmeni*. The formations would be interpreted to determine the source and severity of the attack. But if the oil dispersed and disappeared, she would have a strong *Mati*. In Areti's case, the oil disappeared!

A strong *Mati* would take time and effort to free. Kyria Kaneli knew what methods were needed to release the Evil Eye from Areti and thus alleviate her pain. I was told that in some cases, Kyria Kaneli would use incense and palm branches placed in an incense burner. She would hold the burning essences above the affected person's head, make the sign of the cross and whisper some prayers. In other cases, she would be given a handkerchief from the ill person and tie three knots. Then she would make the sign of the cross in front of the person. Each knot would magically disappear and the handkerchief would become smaller. But Areti's *Mati* required other methods.

Quietly and attentively, I watched Kyria Kaneli carry out her spell-breaking rituals. First of all, she took some palm branches and flowers saved from the symbolic epitaph of Jesus (Good Friday services) and put them into an incense burner together with three seeds of wheat. She said her prayers as she held the incense burner above Areti's head and made the sign of the cross three times. Not only did the seeds begin to move, they started falling out of the incense burner.

"*Panaghia moo!*" she cried out to the Virgin. "A strong *Mati,*" she hissed.

The fight began. Kyria Kaneli struggled to transfer the Evil Eye from Areti's body into her own. Tears formed in her big black eyes as she cried out various incantations to the Holy Virgin. She knelt beside Areti and started to shake. Her hunched body rocked to the rhythms of each Delphic utterance.

I was stunned. I dared not move. Sweat streamed down my forehead as I watched. Kyria Kaneli's left foot stomped against the aged wooden floorboards. A vortex of dust rose from the tiny slits between each plank.

"*Panaghia moo!*" she whispered again and again, calling out the Virgin's name.

The prayers and mystic verses continued, incantations handed down from generation to generation of spell-breakers from Vatika. I listened but I could not understand. I was not meant to understand. I was allowed to witness the powers of the spell-breaker but not to learn her secrets.

Gradually, Kyria Kaneli's body eased into a slow sway. A bit weak at the knees, she stood up, pulled down the scarf tied around her braided hair, and turned her back to Areti. She spit three times into the air saying, "Satan, Get Out!"

She again turned towards Areti and made the sign of the cross above her head holding palm branches and a candle from the resurrection service of Holy Week. She handed me the candle.

"Hold this above her head," she whispered. The candle trembled as I held it.

Kyria Kaneli took out four black stones called *akonia* (stones used to sharpen knives). She said another prayer and started throwing the stones one by one. She threw the first stone behind her back; the second to the right; the third to the left; and the last one again behind her.

She called out, "You are behind me now, Satan."

Areti's eyes slowly opened. Color returned to her once pale skin. The affects of the *Mati* were slowly dissipating. The phantom was gone.

Tears were still running down the face of Kyria Kaneli as she dipped clean muslin strips into cold water to wipe the dust and sweat off her own face. Our whispering voices mingled with the voices of neighboring crickets and cicadas. We heard the distant whine of a dog.

I followed Areti's yiayia into the kitchen where the midday sun reflected against the whitewashed walls of her ancestral village home. She thanked me for being there and handed me a small amulet to wear around my neck. It was a blue glass evil eye.

"Wear it," she insisted. "It will keep the *Mati* away. Areti took her *mati* off before swimming several days ago and forgot to wear it again," she said, as she nodded her head in disappointment. "See what can happen? Never take it off."

The charm is said to "mirror back" the blue of the Evil Eye and thus confound it. The ancient Egyptians used eye shadow and lipstick to prevent the Evil Eye from entering their eyes or mouths. The ancient Greeks and Romans used strange, contorted masks to attract the Evil Eye, absorb its influence and thus protect the person wearing the mask. The very origin of the word "mask" comes from the Greek word *vaska,* also the root of *Vaskania,* and *fascina,* amulets.

Folklore in Vatika cites other ways to avoid or escape the *Mati.* Men wear their undergarments inside out or put oil from the frying pan behind their ears. The black oil from the bottom of a frying pan would leave a smudge on their hands as well. Women would wear a blue bead taken from the reins of a horse. Charms are forever popular. They may be made from candles taken from the epitaph during Holy Week, garlic, a piece of cloth from a dead man, palm branches, incense, a bat's bone, the skin of a snake (*dentrogalia*), or hair from the mane of a black horse. Charms are sewn in a black cloth in the shape of a heart and pinned inside a person's clothes. It is generally thought that evil doesn't approach black colored clothes.

I added the blue-eyed charm to the other symbolic jewelry hanging around my neck. My mother's gold cross and a silver sickle moon have been with me for years, balancing my Christian and pagan worlds. To this day, the Church and popular folklore agree that the curse of the Evil Eye exists, but differ as to how to ward it off. Even though the Orthodox Church claims that the only things that can really protect you are crucifixes and icons from monasteries and churches, and most significantly, true faith, many Greeks hang little blue eyes around their necks and wrists.

I kissed the icon of the Holy Lady goodbye and took the long way home. The landscape was full and fragrant, an Olympian garden of rosemary, lavender, thyme, oregano, and wild marjoram. Passing through olive groves and fields of sage, I smiled as my fingers played with the new charm around my neck. I felt truly protected by my own sacred trinity: a cross, a moon, and now, a *mati*.

The Evil Eye

GAIL STRICKLAND

>~

"'Garlic in your eye!' That's what you say if someone flatters you. Scream silently to yourself, 'Garlic in your eye!' while you stare into that person's eyes, and you will be safe. Well, of course, you should always wear your evil eye." Chrysa, a Greek-American student from Georgetown University, one of our group of women writers visiting Vatika in southern Greece is eager to explain, to help this curious non-Greek find protection with the evil eye charm. She slips a blue bead bracelet onto my wrist and hugs me. For the last half hour, I had been pestering Chrysa. (She would cringe if I say she is beautiful, which she is. I would undoubtedly get a serving of garlic in my blue eye.)

Sitting beside her at a seaside taverna where we are devouring lunch one sunny afternoon, I ask Chrysa and her sister, Alexa, question after question about the evil eye talismans I had been seeing since I arrived in Greece. Beads—deep sea blue surrounded by light blue and white with a black pupil—stared back at me everywhere I traveled.

I had first seen the evil eye charm, *mati* the Greeks call it, in Athens on key chains, necklaces, bracelets and solitary beads displayed for sale along the twisting cobblestone streets of the Plaka, the old marketplace of the city. I swerved across the path, when I caught sight of an entire rack filled with evil eye bracelets. I was determined to ask what they were. A thin, middle-aged woman, her face leathered by sun, took a moment away from pitching olive oil soaps, spices and honey to explain, "*Mati* will protect you. If someone says, 'Oh, I love your dress,' or 'Oh, you are so pretty.' But they are jealous, they do not mean you well. Then you yawn or have headache."

Protection: I like the idea of something which will protect me from others' envy, envy which so often leads to anger and hate. I recognize the danger. I *know* the Evil Eye. In the sixth grade in Georgia, my teacher sent me everyday to the second grade class to tutor the younger children in English. The eyes of all my classmates followed me as I walked out of the room five days a week, walked without a hall pass to the other wing of the school to read aloud Uncle Remus stories and *The Secret Garden*, while my classmates diagrammed sentences. When we displayed our hobbies at back-to-school night, someone pierced my photo with a straight pin right between my eyes. I was proud the teacher chose me to escape the tedium of our classroom, to turn me loose with a room full of eager seven-year-olds to share with them my love of books, but with that pride came the beginning of guilt. Was I too proud? Was it hubris I needed to fear? The "fat head," as one shopkeeper described it later. All I knew when I was twelve years old was their jealousy felt like hate. When I walked that hallway painted institutional green, though I had no name for it, I understood the loneliness of the Evil Eye.

"Don't feel bad if the bracelet breaks." Chrysa spins it on my wrist. "If it shatters, don't give it another thought or worry. It only means that someone tried to give you the Evil Eye and, instead of you getting sick, the beads absorbed the *Mati* and broke. Wearing a *mati* protects you from the *Mati*." She hugs me and encourages me to feel the protection as we both stare out at the brilliant afternoon sea, deep royal blue swirled with aquamarine, fading to the blue of broken Wedgewood pottery, like a shard of crockery slicing into the shallower water of the bay.

I could believe anything as I sip cold white wine and stuff myself on freshly-caught squid, zucchini balls and the best tomatoes I have ever eaten. Besides, I want to believe, to know that friendship and kindness and awareness of flattery's danger can all keep me safe and unafraid.

"I'm confused," I stab another squid tentacle and stuff it in my mouth. "Is *Mati* the eye which protects as well as the eye that makes you sick? They're both the Evil Eye?"

"Yes," Alexa answers, "In earlier days, people believed that eyes have a bad power, especially blue eyes. It goes back to Persia and Egypt, the *Matiazo*. Even the Virgin Mary got the Evil Eye."

I look across the dusty parking lot at a small chapel with white-washed walls, its blue dome topped with a white cross perched solitary beside the sea. It intrigues me that *Mati* is the threat and at the same time *Mati* is peace and protection. I wonder if my protection can be found in the balance between the two.

"Nothing in excess," I mutter mostly to my wine glass.

"What?" Chrysa asks, as she slices her eggplant and looks sideways at me.

"The words of Solon carved on the Temple of Apollo at Delphi," Connie, one of our fearless leaders answers from my left elbow. "Pass me some wine, *parakalo*. That's the deal. Balance, harmony, order, and peace are what we strive for in our daily lives. We understand peace from the horrors of war. We understand the nature of loving from the nature of hating."

No wonder I am fascinated with the Evil Eye. Threat. Protection. The catch of breath, of balance in-between the two, is what I have been seeking for years. The exterior threat of the Evil Eye is easy to comprehend, but I begin to wonder how much of the threat of *Mati* is within. Like the squid, am I hiding from shadows in the water? Do I make myself sick with my own fear?

I stab another piece of squid and think about the fisherman pounding it against the rocks so it will release its ink, the ink it uses for protection—a black, sinuous cloud which envelopes it to obscure it from enemies—or presumed enemies. Sometimes it is only a shadow overhead. I know the feeling. How many times have

I felt like I was being attacked, or worse yet, feared attack was imminent and run to hide? The squid's other great defense is hiding in tiny rock crevices safe from a larger enemy. At least a squid has a fairly good idea whose teeth are about to devour it. I often think that most of my enemies are fantasies of my own fears.

Like shadows of sharks circling around me, the talk of the Evil Eye has brought back memories: My first husband telling me I have "a nice nose" while I know he is leaving me for another woman. A friend believing I give her the Evil Eye when I compliment her two little girls, because I have been infertile for four years. And the friend who has no college degree, but can do anything she tries—gourmet cooking, clothing design, acting, singing—but she mistrusts my words of praise and our friendship is shattered for years. And what about the friend who asks me to write a screenplay adaptation of her novel? She declares it is "wonderful, just what she wants," but does not mention it exists when a producer asks if he can make a movie based on her book. No, she is jealous because she thinks her boyfriend is flirting with me.

As if reading my thoughts, Chrysa reaches for the plate piled high with rusk (dried bread) and muses out loud, "People who are sensitive are especially susceptible to the Evil Eye." I can believe that.

"Gail, have you finished your first story?" I flinch as Linda, one of the instructors, asks. She is really just making conversation, but my mind turns to the story I'm writing and what the other writers will think of it. If they like it, I'll probably spend the next couple of days trying to re-create what I think they like. If they don't—well, that's simple. I'll probably just freeze up and not be able to write another word. It amazes me once again to realize how praise can be just as deadly as criticism. Look at all the trouble caused by Paris declaring Aphrodite was the "most beautiful goddess of all!" It wasn't Helen who launched a thousand ships to start the ten-year Trojan War. It was praise, jealousy: the Evil Eye.

A few days later, beneath a hot Aegean sun, we travel by taxi. Actually I'm in Connie's car, singing along with Janis Joplin and The Righteous Brothers at the top of our lungs, while we wind through villages where old men seated in the shade of grape arbors stare at us as we barrel past. Midday we arrive at Monemvasia, a walled fortress city surrounded by thick stone walls and the sea, almost unassailable. I'm still asking everyone I meet about the Evil Eye. Tasia, a gifted jewelry designer, works silver and stones and gold into intricate patterns taken from Aghia Sophia: Byzantine designs, Moorish designs, and patterns as old as the sea waves, designs borrowed from all the empires who claimed this jutting Greek fortress. She talks about the invaders, the blue-eyed threat of the Dorian invasion, the wild hoards from the north who conquered the Mycenaeans thousands of years ago. Centuries later, other blue-eyed conquerors came, the Nazis. They all loved the dusty olive trees, the harmony and simplicity that is the Greek land, the Greek spirit. Then they claimed it for their own. First praise, then possession. No wonder the Greeks wear the evil eye. Beware those who covet that which is Greek, the Greek spirit, for they may return to claim it as their own.

For a second Tasia looks away from my blue eyes, pauses, then looks back up again and smiles. "I don't really believe in the Evil

Eye." She brings her hands up and wipes the glass counter with a soft cloth, gathers up some silver chains left there, closes the velvet case. "I don't really believe, except my boy, he is so beautiful. Everyone keeps stopping me to tell me how beautiful he is. I do not want him to get the Evil Eye. The fat head. So I sew a *mati* into the collar of his shirt. I don't really believe, but . . ."

She turns away to help another customer and when she comes back to talk to me, she tells me the protection of the Evil Eye comes from ancient times, perhaps from "grey-eyed Athena" or the eyes of her owl, protector of wisdom. What is the *Mati's* wisdom? I look deep into this mother's dark eyes and feel her love for her son. My daughter had serious asthma her entire childhood. There were the trips to the emergency room, sleepless nights listening to her rough breathing. I know a mother's desire to protect. I would have sewn a *mati* into the sleeve of my daughter's blouse if I'd known. I buy a lovely blue eye from Tasia and a delicate silver chain to bring home as a present to my daughter.

I wish it could be so simple for me. I wish I could buy a charm, accept a bracelet, just believe they will keep me safe. But I think what it really comes down to is my fear. Praise, rejection, it all throws me off balance.

Later in the evening, I pick up my yellow notebook and walk down the narrow white staircase which leads from my upstairs bedroom to the living room below. The other writers are gathered on benches and chairs around a white stucco fireplace decorated with shells, stones, and ancient potshards spit back by the sea. I am the last to arrive, since I have been traveling with a hurt knee and am a little slow. As I descend into view, they look up at me and smile. That smile envelopes me, welcomes me to their circle. I begin to understand what Chrysa, Alexa, Connie, and Tasia were telling me, "Wear the charm, blue, coral, it doesn't matter what color."

Chrysa said it back at the taverna, "The power of the *Mati* kept you safe." *Mati* translated means "eye." The answer was there for me all along, I just had not understood. *Mati* is not worn to look within and worry our losses and fears like a dog worrying a bone, it is to look back at the world and see it truly. The power of *Mati* protects us because it frees us to see that we are, after all, only human. We hurt each other with our jealousies and fears. Sometimes we mean to, sometimes we don't, but beyond those dividing jealousies is the divine spark that unites us all. I take the last step and join their circle. I still hope they will like my story, but just in case they give me a hard time, there's always "Garlic in your eye!"

NOTE ABOUT "WHAT THE SHEPHERD SAW"

"The poet would say 'there was. . .they were. . .' But the shepherd says he lives, he is, he does. . .The poet is always a thousand years too late—and blind to boot. The shepherd is eternal, an earth-bound spirit, a renunciator. On these hillsides forever and ever there will be the shepherd with his flock: he will survive everything, including the tradition of all that ever was."

—HENRY MILLER, *THE COLOSSUS OF MAROUSSI*

Early in the twentieth century a shepherd, Kostas Stivalktas Mbougas, was tending his sheep in the hot, rocky hills of Vatika near the town of Kastania. Needing water, he discovered bees swarming out of a crack in a rock, and wondered if water lay inside the hill. He dug open the crack and, carefully lowering himself into the hole, discovered an astonishing limestone cave with splendid stalactites and stalagmites of wondrous colors and shapes. Approximately three million years old, the cave comprises fifteen hundred square meters in eighteen chambers and extends thirty meters deep in the ground. After his discovery, Kostas Mbougas hid the entrance to the cave, keeping private his source of water.

In 1958, having seen a television show about the important discovery of a similar cave in Greece, Mbougas realized "his" cave might have further value. After study by scientists, and construction of ninety-three meters of paved walkways, Mbougas' cave was opened to the public, for guided tours only. It is now known as the Cave of Aghios Andreas or the Cave of Kastania.

What the Shepherd Saw

Seeking only water
    where the bees swarmed
        beneath ground,
the shepherd cracked
the earth open
until he hit light
    that slit
        the cave
— the shape of God's mind—
where God's dreams dripped
    slowly
into pillars of thought.

He saw how the world began:
    pillars of salt,
        mountains of crystal
            the shape of things to come.

This was the darkness before darkness,
the light before light.
This was where the mist from God's breath,
    sliver,
        rose,
            blue,
                gold,

colored the world
while She was still dreaming
the gods to be.

This was the underworld
before the underworld,
before Hades knew the dark,
before Demeter knew sorrow,
and Persephone knew spring.

This was the cave
before Plato's cave,
    before reality played
      with light
        and shadow.

This was the silence
before sound,
    where pale white spiders
      blind and deaf
        spun
          translucent webs
   in those ages
     measureless to man,
before Homer,
   the blind musician
sang.

These were the forms of life before being:
columns, towers, minarets,
herds of elephants,
a cluster of grapes,
a Chinese maiden,
a Buddha.

These were the intentions of God
before one became many:
those three Wise Men on a camel,
those cathedrals of ice and stone,
a Holy Mother and Child,
a sign of the Cross
the shapes of hope
and death,
the slant of prayer.

This is what the shepherd saw.
Then
a bee buzzed by,
a bell rang out loud,
or a sheep bleated from afar.
And he quickly closed the cave.

—Joanna Biggar

Goat Song

CATHERINE PYKE

>

No one saw it but me. We were on our way to the cave of Kastania. Two taxis and a jeep drove in caravan ascending a steep, winding road high above the Bay of Neapolis. Terraced groves of olive trees formed semicircular rings in volcanic rock as far as the eye could see. As we rounded a hairpin bend in the road, I saw it—the remnants of an ancient Greek theatre. Stones, nearly covered in wild grasses, formed concentric half-rings fanning upward against the mountainside. I burst with excitement, but no one in the jeep could hear me. Janis Joplin's music blared as we neared the peak of the mountain, my four traveling companions singing along at the top of their lungs of freedom and Bobby McGee. I didn't think I cared for Janis Joplin's music, but I remembered that she'd once lived in the town of Larkspur where I now live. This, combined with my excitement at discovering the theatre I'd hoped I'd find in the Peloponnese, made me feel the passion in her voice for the first time.

I tapped our driver on the shoulder. "Did you see the ancient Greek theatre?"

"I'm driving," she said, "You're seeing things."

The nearest known theatre was in Epidaurus, a drive of several hours away. Until recently, it was a fully-functioning theatre, holding live performances for nearly 14,000, with acoustics so perfect you could hear a pin fall in the orchestra from the theatre's most remote seats. Epidaurus was closed this summer for extensive renovations, the victim of damage from years of high-heeled shoes and destructive bubble gum that threaten to ruin this sparkling jewel of a theatre built in the early third century B.C. There was virtually no chance I'd be able to see the ancient Greek theatre I'd hoped to see on this trip. And yet I knew that the cult of Dionysus flourished everywhere in Greece. It seemed perfectly logical to me that the ruins of theatres, as common in their day as the village church, might be hidden by olive groves and vegetation overtaking the ancient terraces that run along the descending mountainsides we passed on our daily excursions.

As the jeep neared the peak of the mountain, six black, horned goats leaped out onto the dirt road and stopped traffic. Whenever I see a goat, I feel certain Dionysus is present. The word tragedy means "goat song." The beginnings of theatre were found in choral songs celebrating Dionysus, when a goat, thought to embody the god, was torn to pieces and given as a prize to the creator of the best song in his honor. Plays sponsored by the state were presented at religious festivals celebrating the god. During the most famous one, the spring festival of Dionysus, business as usual shut down. The courts were closed, prisoners were released and women as well as men attended free plays and rituals lasting five days to celebrate the god. Songs told of heroic events, dramatizing incidents in the life of Dionysus, the god of, among other things, winemaking. From religious rituals in the god's honor, both tragedy and its bawdy cousin, comedy, mimicking gestures to stimulate the fertility of the earth, were born. Now there was no doubt in my mind, I had seen the ruins of an ancient Greek theatre.

We had been bumping along a rugged, unpaved road, on our way to an underground cave. Early in the 1900's, a shepherd watched bees entering a crack in the rocks in his fields near the village of Saint Andrew. When the bees resurfaced, he thought they looked refreshed. It occurred to him that the bees were going into the earth for water. Desperate for water himself, he followed the bees through the open fissure. To the shepherd's astonishment, he encountered a rare cave, full of stalactites and stalagmites, more than three million years old. Our group walked through the cave, cooled by the occasional drip from a stalactite, which I learned hang down from the cave's ceiling, versus the stalagmite that builds up from its floor. The colors were dazzling, the shapes even more so, offering symbols suggestive of religious icons, like the three Magi. There is only one living creature, a blind spider, which makes its home in the cave. Our guide shined a flashlight on the many-legged albino creature, seemingly content to live alone in darkness.

Wandering past the mysterious forms, this dark cavern seemed to me like the Greek mythological Underworld as I'd imagined it. Later, I asked Professor Thanasis Maskaleris, who had been talking with us about Dionysus, if the caves were thought to be representative of the Underworld.

"No, not at all," he insisted. "The caves speak of the earth. They are about life, not death."

I learned that caves celebrate Demeter, the goddess of the Earth. I also learned that Demeter and Dionysus were worshiped together, both divinities of the gifts of the earth, equally present in the breaking of bread and the drinking of wine.

Walking through the cave, I realized how trapped I am in my own way of looking at things. Like the humans living in an underground den that Plato speaks of in his Allegory of the Cave (*The Republic*, Book VII), most of us live in a world of relative ignorance. We mistake shadows for reality. When we are finally released from the cave to see the truth, we are slow to accept it. Most of the time, I am content to see the world through rose-colored glasses, seeing what I wish to see. But it struck me, walking through that cave, that one can just as easily dismiss an actual possibility, like the sight of a ruined ancient Greek theatre, by distrusting what the eyes and mind perceive.

Emerging from the cave, I asked our tour guide if she was aware of any nearby ruins of an ancient theatre.

"No," she laughed, "No theatres here."

Something inside of me refused to believe her.

With the possible exception of that blind spider, few Greeks are content to live alone in darkness, trapped within the confines of their own mind. The Greeks' nature requires them to escape the cave, to come together to celebrate life in its most extreme and hilarious moments. The experience of witnessing a play in an outdoor ancient Greek theatre must have been like what most of us feel when we sit in a baseball stadium on a hot summer day. Listening to the roar of the audience, feeling the sun warm our skin, we are one with the exhilaration of the crowd.

There were three, perhaps four male actors who took on a variety of roles in a Greek play. The actors wore masks that stared out at the audience in expressions of constant horror or amusement, allowing them to take on both male and female roles. A chorus of busybodies hung around, singing or offering gossip and commentary on the happenings of the play. Not advancing the plot, the members of the chorus occupied a curious role. Like callers-in to The Larry King Show, they seemingly enjoyed and drew moral lessons voyeuristically from tragic lives splayed out for communal consumption like a fast food banquet.

How can it be that the suffering of others brings the Greek in all of us pleasure?

In the *Poetics,* Aristotle suggests that the psychological processes that come over us as we watch tragedy offer an emotional catharsis. My own unscholarly view is that observing tragedy offers lessons that teach us how to live our own lives more fully, in a more meaningful way. While I feel slightly guilty reading obituaries of people I have never known, there is no sense of shame in witnessing a tragic play. We revel, observing the passionate sufferings of people we will never know, for a rational, nearly noble reason. Tragedy appeals to us, I believe, because in everything we observe or contemplate, we are constantly measuring our lives against others, attempting to gain perspective on what it is to be human, to understand the possibilities of our short time on earth. We observe tragedy to try to learn to be better people. Similarly, comedy appeals because it's comforting somehow to feel that others are as flawed, accident prone and ridiculous as ourselves, possibly even more so.

Later in the day, as our group wandered lost through a farmer's meadow, in search of a petrified forest we had already passed, we came upon a horrifying sight.

"Oh, no," Linda gasped, spying the severed head of a goat placed high in the branch of a tree.

We all stared at the goat's head, wondering how it got there, pondering its meaning. Had the head been placed in the tree by a farmer to dry? Unlikely, someone observed, noting that Greeks like to eat the whole goat, including the head. A variation on a traditional expression goes something like, "If you're going to eat the goat, why stop at the tail?"

Gail wondered if the severed head of the goat in the tree had a mysterious, slightly dark religious meaning. Was it some sort of Dionysian ritual? Pondering the severed head, it occurred to me that the sight was both tragic and funny, in a twisted sort of way. The goat had a comical look on its face, as if it were laughing at us, hopelessly lost in a farmer's fields.

Later that night, as we drank wine and ate octopus and danced like the crazed women, the Meanads who followed Dionysus around in a wine-frenzied state, I realized that in Greece, the theatre is everywhere. It is in the mountain terraces, the copious food, the impressionistic glow of olive grove and glittering sea that one feels it, imbibing wine or stone cold sober. At the end of our journey, as we embarked on the five-hour long taxi ride back to Athens and rounded the curve of a road above a seaside village, yet another herd of goats leaped out onto the road. The goats stopped us again with a final gentle reminder, as if we needed it, that in Greece, the theatre is everywhere. It is the spirit of life itself.

On the Steps of Aghios Nektarios

ALEXA TSAKOPOULOS

⤳

There is a church above a nightclub in Neapoli, Greece. As I trudged up the cement path, securing my toes on the tight ridges to keep my balance, the wind grew stronger.

"Sarah," I sang in a mock operatic tone, "hurry up you old goof, we have to make it back to town by four o'clock. And at the rate we're climbing, we won't even make it up to the church by that time." It was the summer before my sixteenth birthday, a carefree summer filled with laughter.

"Alexa," Sarah squeezed the air out of her lungs to utter my name. I collapsed on the cement walkway, my eyes meeting hers, recognizing with a grin how incredibly out of shape we both were.

We rested against the cement wall as our heart rates slowed from a gallop to a trot.

"If two fifteen-year-olds cannot even climb up this hill," I mumbled, "how in God's name do the little old ladies do it?" Sarah and I giggled at the thought, as we sprawled out on the steep hillside.

Looking at the sky, I let the air surge into my lungs, breathing slowly in through my nose and out through my mouth. I inhaled a strange, familiar scent.

I recognized it: chamomile. I immediately thought about my grandmother. I wondered what she was doing at that moment. The warm fragrance eased the pain in my head, and I longed for the chamomile tea my grandmother made as a cure for any ailment.

I cherish the sensations that bring her back to me: chamomile tea, plates of kiwi and strawberries with sugar, trips to the opera, feeding the seagulls in the Marina, eating bagels with cream cheese, watching *Bye Bye Birdie* in the morning.

As a third grader, my grandmother would treat me to Baskin Robbins' ice cream every Sunday: mint chocolate chip on a sugar cone. Later on, as a freshman in high school, my priorities skewed. My attention was focused on my girlfriends and boys, boys, boys. I reluctantly accompanied my grandmother to Baskin Robbins for our weekly ritual, as I thought of what I was going to wear that evening to the school dance. Absorbed by teen preoccupations, I failed to cherish that moment—and many other moments—with my ailing, aging grandmother.

My grandmother stopped coming to Greece when the long flights became hard for her to endure. It was strange for me to be in her village when she was at home in California. I was constantly reminded of her: the tiny beach umbrellas that lined the shore; the humid mist that gently lingered over the Aegean; and the faces of my many local relatives. Even panting my way to the top of the hill, I could not help thinking of her.

Sarah grabbed my hands and pulled me up from the cement, the sweat on our skin making it difficult to hold on. Finally, we came face to face with the bold cross standing proud atop the cream dome. We were in awe of the beauty of the church. Its slender arches and white marble steps whispered, "Come rest in my shade, feel the cool marble on your skin."

Sarah and I clambered up the elegant steps. A klutz, I stumbled on the last one, falling to my knees. Sarah chortled. I smiled, embarrassed. I crawled over to the side of the marble steps, letting my feet dangle over the edge. Sarah walked over and slowly slipped her feet over the edge of the marble, too, as if she were submerging her feet in a cold swimming pool. We sat for a moment in silence.

The Church of Aghios Nektarios (Saint Nektarios) was built to honor the saint. Unlike other popular Greek saints, Aghios Nektarios was not a martyr. He did not withdraw to a hermitage, or contend with cruel persecution or tragic torture. He lived his life as a continuous doxology to God. He worked tirelessly to benefit a society suffering from moral and religious dilemmas. The town folk of Neapoli said that "he had the form of man, but lived like an angel." The church is a breathtaking tribute to the man, or perhaps I should say, the angel.

"I'd like to get married in a church just like this; simple and beautiful, maybe in Kentucky," Sarah said looking into the distance, her deep green eyes grazing the horizon.

"What about you?"

I thought about it for a moment and replied, "There is a tiny church in my Dad's village on top of this huge mountain. It can only fit about five people, but it's charming, and means a lot to me. But with all my relatives, I have to have it in a big church somewhere." Tilting my head back for a moment until I could see the church doors upside-down, I rocked my head back up. "Maybe here," I thought out loud.

The sun was dancing along the majestic arch curving away from the bluest of skies towards the water's edge. "We should get going," I said, as Sarah jumped off of the cold, marble step.

While Sarah slowly descended the hill, I stopped to take in the breathtaking view of the Neapolis Bay and the whitewashed houses scattered across this familiar, familial landscape. Leaving the church, I came across a quote from Saint Nektarios himself, "Man is not only reason, but also heart." I learned that lesson, not from a great saint, but from my loving grandmother.

Cultivating Olives

BARBARA J. EUSER

༃

"All set to go then, dear?" the burly, bearded Greek taxi driver cheerfully called out to me in broad Australian. Yiannis is a native-born Greek, but he spent from ages eight to eighteen in Australia. When he returned to Greece as a young man, he decided to stay. He is a member of the Greek diaspora: Greeks who have spent a few years, or whose families have spent a generation or two, living abroad, but who ultimately return to this dry, rock-strewn mountainous land.

Appearances are deceiving. Yiannis only drives his taxi when he is not tending his groves of olives: one thousand trees in five separate plots around Neapoli. Yiannis is an olive grower disguised as a taxi driver. For five hours, as he drove expertly, speedily through Sparta, Tripoli, and Corinth to Athens, he talked about his olive trees, harvesting his crop, and the cooperative olive oil press.

In a way, Yiannis was telling me a familiar tale. My father was a grower. He was born in Holland, where his family had a market garden and grew vegetables under Dutch lights and in greenhouses. After he emigrated to the United States at the age of twenty-three, he worked on a farm, then started his own plant nursery. Eventually, he built eleven acres of greenhouses and grew carnations and roses commercially. He sold his flowers through a wholesalers' cooperative. I identified with Yiannis' stories about weather, pests, and marketing his crop.

Farming runs in families. Yiannis inherited his olive trees from his father. His plots are separated because over time a family's land is divided between children, then transferred between relatives, until what any one person owns is a hodgepodge of small properties. Having a five-piece farm is inefficient. Yiannis described the difficulties, "I have to drive between them, so time I could be working, I am on the road, traveling from one plot to another. I have to have five buildings for tools and equipment. If I don't want to carry all my tools with me, I have to have five different sets."

Small and large olive groves form silver-leaved patches in the landscape quilt of Vatika. But the hundreds of thousands of olive trees that thrive in Greece are not native species. There are several theories about their origins. Some scientists believe olive trees originated in Asia Minor; other scientists claim they originated in the Caucasus Mountains. Olive trees appear to have spread over time from Syria towards Greece by way of Anatolia. By the sixteenth century B.C., the Phoenicians spread olive trees throughout the Greek islands. By the twelfth century B.C., olive trees were growing on the Greek mainland. By the fourth century B.C., the importance of olive cultivation had increased to a point that Solon issued decrees regulating the planting of olive trees.

Olive trees married happily into the local soil and climactic conditions. The so-called Mediterranean climate exists in only a few places in the world outside the basin of the Mediterranean Sea: the west coast of Australia, the west coast of South Africa and the west coast of the United States around San Francisco Bay. It is characterized by cool, rainy winters, and hot, dry summers. In a Mediterranean climate, one must plant in the fall to take advantage of the rainy season. Plants planted in late spring will suffer from the immediate stress of the summer drought. Transplants must be planted with these conditions in mind.

I, too, am a transplant here. In my life, I have moved many times. As a Foreign Service officer, I moved with my husband and two daughters from Colorado to Washington, D.C., to Guangzhou, China, back to Washington, D.C., and to Paris, France. Then my family tired of moving and we settled near my husband's family outside San Francisco. Now our children are grown. My husband has returned to his roots in Marin County. But I have never felt at home there. When we lived in Paris, I discovered I prefer to live in Europe. Now in Greece, I have found a location that suits me. Cities and towns alike are characterized by neighborhoods. Virtually everything one needs can be found within walking distance. I have found an intellectual climate conducive to creativity and a physical climate conducive to health. In Neapoli, I write every morning and swim in the clear, cool Aegean every afternoon. Locals enjoy their *banio*, or daily swim, before a mid-afternoon meal and *mesimeri*, a late afternoon nap. Evenings are for visiting with friends and late dinners under the stars. Like the olive trees, I have found a climate where I can thrive.

Olive trees are now an inherent part of Greek culture and cuisine. Whenever oil is needed in cooking, olive oil is used, from deep-frying french-fries, to oil-and-lemon fish sauce, to tangy salad dressings. According to Sylvia, mother of three, a Greek family of five uses approximately one hundred and twenty kilos of olive oil each year. That translates into one hundred and thirty-three liters, or over two liters of olive oil per person per month. Olive oil is used in soap and soothing lotions. The curved-grained wood is used to fashion items from kitchen utensils to furniture.

Most every family in Vatika has a few olive trees. They may be grown on a terrace outside the front door, or on an inherited piece of property known only to initiates. When the olives are ripe, the branches can be beaten with rakes and olives will drop onto a cloth placed beneath the trees. The best olives are saved for the table. They are washed, then slit open, so the salt and vinegar brine they are placed in can penetrate and preserve them. After several days, they can be removed from the brine, covered in olive oil and refrigerated. Other more sophisticated recipes include drying the brine-preserved olives with aromatic herbs.

The rest of the olives from a family's trees are taken to the local coop. The traditional olive press in Kriovrissis on the hillside above Neapoli consisted of two stones turned by donkeys harnessed in traces. The building still stands, but the millstones are gone. The olive press in use today is located in Pandanassa. Its stainless steel presses are powered by electricity. But the outcome is the same: kilos of green-gold olive oil.

I, too, have a product emerging from my time in Greece: writing. First, essays on gardening in the now-familiar Mediterranean climate, but in a place far-removed from San Francisco Bay. Then a screenplay I had thought of for years, but had never written down. Now this anthology of essays by writers, all inspired by the same climate, during our workshop in Vatika. What is it about this environment, one that appears so rocky and desolate, yet results in such fecundity?

When a family takes its bounty of olives to the cooperative press, the olives are weighed. For every kilo weighed in, the family receives a certain amount of oil in return, minus a commission of oil paid to the cooperative for its services.

A commercial grower like Yiannis does the same thing. He takes his harvested olives to the press to be weighed then transformed into oil. But rather than taking his oil home, the cooperative credits the grower with a certain number of kilos to be sold. The oil is sold at auction. Buyers are an international crowd. Some come from Italy. These buyers are commercial olive oil producers themselves who buy the rich Greek oil to add flavor to the lighter Italian oil. According to Yiannis, the Italians use a ratio of one part Greek oil to nine parts Italian oil to achieve the flavor they desire. The oil is marketed as Italian oil, though it has been flavor-enhanced.

"Considering we produce the best olive oil, we don't make as much money as we should," Yiannis complained.

I commiserated with him. "I think it's a marketing problem. Greek olive oil could be marketed as the highest end olive oil, so rich in flavor you only need to add a little bit to your salads to get fantastic taste. You should be getting a premium price for your oil. But, of course, that would require a whole marketing campaign. And who would pay for it? The coop?" I asked.

"Not bloody likely," came the response.

Inwardly, I smiled. The stories written for this anthology are rich and full of individual flavor. Each writer found nourishment for her work from instructors and fellow participants, and inspiration from the land itself. And marketing the final product will be an issue of concern for me, just as it is for Yiannis.

Another local olive grower, Kosta, was kind enough to take me to visit his olive grove. Kosta also has a day job: a thriving practice as a physical therapist. He took me to his family's farm where he cultivates almost nine hundred olive trees. In some of his groves, one-inch diameter black plastic pipes festooned the trees, stretching from the branches of one tree to the next. "What are those pipes for?" I asked.

"Irrigation," Kosta explained. He took me to the pump house for the well his father drilled. He poured twenty liters of diesel fuel into the engine that powers the pump. He added water to the radiator, then checked the oil. He turned the pump engine on, then opened the valves on four-inch black plastic pipes that carried the water to the smaller pipes hanging from the trees.

In some sections of Kosta's olive grove, the plastic pipes run along the ground, just as they do in my garden in California. The olive trees can obviously survive without irrigation, but with some added water they will increase their yield.

"When is the olive harvest?" I asked.

"In the fall," Kosta replied. "Usually mid-October. We have a saying here that when the olives are yellow, they are ready to pick. But I also have a few trees of Kalamata olives for the table. Those olives aren't ripe until they are black. Olive trees bloom in late April. When the trees are blooming, they look white instead of green. The fruit sets in early summer. Then, of course, pests may attack, especially flies. We call them *dakos*. The flies lay their eggs in the young olives, then when the eggs hatch, the larvae eat the olives from the inside." He searched a tree for an infected olive. He showed me the black spot on the outside of the olive that indicated a fly had laid its eggs there. He opened the olive with his fingernail and traced the path of the larvae.

"What can you do about that?" I asked.

"First, we hang traps in the trees. See those plastic bottles hanging from the branches?"

I saw gallon-size white plastic bottles hanging from occasional trees.

"Those contain a pheromone that attracts the flies. They fly into the bottle and drown. But the bottles are just indicators of the fly population. If I find more than ten drowned flies, then I have to spray the trees with insecticide. If I find just a few flies in the bottle, I know there will be some damage to the crop, but I can tolerate that. I prefer not to spray."

"After the harvest, I put my trees to bed," Kosta continued. "I prune out dead branches and crossing branches and generally shape the trees. Then I mulch around the base of the trunks. So next year we can start all over again."

This is the yearly cycle of production. In my work, there is a cycle of production, too. The workshop cycle starts in the fall, with the inspiration for next summer, followed by planning and organizing in winter and spring. In summer, the workshop flowers: in 2005 in the south of France, in 2006 in the south of Greece. Then the fruit—the essays—must ripen through writing, editing and rewriting, before the final product, the anthology, appears. And, as with the olive trees, as soon as the harvest is complete, the cycle begins again.

Don't Flush!

LINDA JUE

❧

"Don't flush." As I crunched down to examine the sign more carefully, I could feel the slightest twinge beginning to stir in my chest. Once again, my Yankee sensibilities were about to be challenged.

Posted above the toilet paper roll in the women's restroom in a busy Athens cafe, a small sign grabbed my attention with its no-nonsense command—in giant red letters, no less:

DON'T FLUSH.
PLACE PAPER IN RECEPTACLE
PROVIDED FOR THE PURPOSE.

I looked down in front of me to see a dismally tiny trashcan. It didn't look like it could possibly accommodate more than a handful of people, much less the dozens who likely pass through during the day.

"What!" I exclaimed. "They want me to put this in THAT??"

I had just landed in Greece a few hours earlier. Culture shock had set in. Up until that moment, I hadn't really absorbed the fact that I was no longer "in Kansas." I'd had no trouble negotiating the buses and taxis to get to my destination from the airport. Handling the currency conversion wasn't a problem. Despite the total incomprehensibility of the language to my eyes and ears (it truly was all Greek to me), there seemed to be plenty of English speakers around to assist me. Even the city streets looked like they could have been found in any outer New York borough. Nothing so far had appeared particularly strange. It was almost disappointing.

But then I'd forgotten about the toilets—always the most intimate test of one's adaptability when traveling. Observing the mild horror I was trying to suppress in that Athens water closet, I realized that middle age and middle-class life had caught up with me. All those years of globetrotting—of opening up not only to other cultures but to their plumbing facilities as well—seemed to have gone down the . . . yes, toilet.

Creeping finicky-ness had finally found its toehold, after decades of retreat from ideological harangues about the American fixation with proper flushies. I could hear European friends of long ago deriding our "see no evil, hear no evil, speak no evil" stance toward our bodily functions. To which I replied at the time, "Hey, blame it on the Puritans, who, by the way, happened to have come from England."

Eventually my friends' taunts, along with repeated exposure to the world's latrines, did wield their influence. I'd managed to acquire a more sanguine perspective about the countless styles of human elimination. In fact, toilets I had known and loved—not—became the source of many humorous anecdotes. I would regale my friends with stories of toilet paper in 1970's London that had imprinted on every rough-hewn sheet, "Now wash your hands, please." Or the pit toilets in Thailand that so graciously provided footprints astride the opening, as if figuring out where to plant one's feet was the only impediment to using the damn things. Or the German toilets with platforms built inside the bowls to catch That Which Shall Not Be Named before it hit the water.

My favorite toilet of all was a Japanese contraption outfitted with every manner of button to personalize your bathroom experience. You could warm the seat to your heart's desire. You could rinse your tushie without bothering to get up. You could even wash your hands courtesy of the mini-sink built onto the tank for your convenience. This baby could do everything but bow.

Yet there I was, in the summer of 2006, contemplating Greek toilet habits with dismay. My, how times had changed. But one can linger only so long on these hygienic profundities when there's a line of people literally knocking at your door.

Noticing the little foot pedal at the base of the receptacle, I breathed a minor sigh of relief. "Good," I thought. "At least I don't have to touch the thing with my hands." Ever so gingerly, I stepped on the pedal just enough to partially raise the lid. No way would I allow myself a full view of the contents. Slowly, I inched my hand into the opening, laboring not to touch the rim of the can. Or, God forbid, anything else. I peeked in just long enough to make sure it wasn't full; I don't know what I would have done if it had been. Then, I made my drop. I yanked my hand out so quickly that I startled myself.

"Christ," I muttered, exasperated. "I've got two more weeks of this."

I exited the WC perturbed that my backsliding anal retentiveness could ruin my trip. After all, I had come to Greece for loftier pursuits. Fourteen writers and myself were about to convene for ten days to produce a collection of essays about the Vatika region, located on the southernmost tip of the Peloponnese. We would publish these essays later in the fall as a book about traveling off the beaten path in Greece. It would be an ambitious venture among mostly strangers, half of whom had never set foot in Greece before.

I fretted that as we toured various sights on the peninsula, there would be no escaping the inevitable. When one had to go, one had to go. Nonetheless, I swore not to let atavistic tendencies play havoc with my Aegean adventures.

The first hint that I was not alone in my preoccupations occurred that same evening. Several of us were staying in the apartment of one of the group's organizers, Connie, a lively Greek American from San Francisco who had moved to Athens nearly three decades earlier. Scrutinizing the same ridiculously small waste can in Connie's bathroom, the journalist in me came out. My mind raced with questions: Why are those cans so small? What *do* they do with all that used TP? Why can't we flush the paper?

Images of piles of unflushed TP occupying landfills all over Greece sent shudders through me. What about the biohazard issues, I wondered, when ten million people are wiping their behinds several times a day every single day? The idea of sanitation workers handling trash filled with the remains of people's *caca* so revolted me that it sent my own bowels on strike.

Since Connie had left for the Vatika before our arrival, I couldn't get any answers from her. Instead, I decided to find out if any of my companions were experiencing the same qualms. Spotting Mary Jean and Ann in the hallway, I announced, "Uhmm, I've got a personal hygiene question."

"Yeah?" said M.J., as they both looked at me expectantly.

"Well . . . when we have our, uh, bowel movements? Are we actually supposed to, uh, put the paper in the can?"

M.J. just shrugged. "What else can we do?"

But Ann replied, "I don't know. I'm avoiding the whole question by not going."

In the following days, I would discover that nearly half our group—all women, as it turned out—harbored some misgivings about the toilets. On the van ride down from Athens to the village of Mesochori, our base for the duration, we stopped in Sparta for lunch. Jokingly, I asked one of my lunch mates to report back on the condition of the facilities at the restaurant. To my surprise, it was a request that was taken quite seriously. Several others were hesitant to go until they heard that the bathrooms were habitable. Part of the reluctance stemmed from the usual garden-variety aversion to public toilets everywhere. But perhaps more pertinently, we seemed to be collectively avoiding those stunted trashcans, especially if they might be spilling over their contents.

Our home for the next nine days was a villa clinging to a hillside overlooking the Aegean Sea. Built by our host, Virginia, the house looked like the perfect candidate for a *Condé Nast Traveler* spread. Whitewashed, accented with dark wooden doors and windows, surrounded by garden patios and terraces looking out to the water, the house, like its owner, instantly welcomed us into its warm embrace. Inside, we found a home filled with Greek country furnishings arranged with an unpretentious elegance. Every room offered expansive views out to the sea. An immediate ease began to settle in among us, as if we had arrived at our own exclusive sanctuary.

Ann and I teamed up to occupy the bottom floor of a two-level cottage. It appeared to be the largest of all the bedrooms, furnished with a kitchenette, a dining/writing table, a small cot, a roomy bathroom, and a long divan that functioned as both couch and bed. Of course, the best amenity was the view out the door. Staring at the Aegean, I was stunned by the water's legendary hue: a deep, clear sapphire that glittered relentlessly under the summer sun. The afternoon light shone a hazy brilliance that nearly blinded me. And the cicadas. They were everywhere, their roar at times reaching a deafening crescendo. For the first time in weeks, my body began to unwind. This is why I came to Greece, I reminded myself.

As sublime as our surroundings were, however, I still had trouble getting used to those receptacles. Apparently, so did others. Casual conversations about the bathrooms over the next couple days would surface private anxieties. One person seriously considered going home because she just couldn't deal with the local custom. Another had "forgotten" to use the waste can and stopped up the system, requiring Virginia to call a plumber. To make matters worse, we were responsible for emptying out those cans when they became full. Virginia showed Ann how to bundle up the trash in plastic bags and then hang them from the trees at the back of the house. That way, critters wouldn't explore the contents before garbage day. Somehow I couldn't imagine any less incentive for a gaggle of constipated, hyper-sanitary phobics to fill up their trashcans.

Fortunately, we had other priorities to focus on besides our ambivalent relationship with the Greek toilet. We had to get to know Vatika in a hurry and then write about it. Connie and Barbara, the driving force behind this whole caper, had organized a native's tour of the region. We took excursions to nearby sites frequented mostly by locals. We hiked the hills and swam in the sea. We became acquainted with the area's inhabitants. We sampled ouzo and inhaled Virginia's cooking. Barbara had even arranged our own personal wine tasting lecture and dinner at a vineyard in Neapoli, the fishing town just down the road from Mesochori.

With a couple of exceptions, we saw no other foreigners wherever we went. Guidebooks don't say much about this part of the Peloponnese except that it is the departure point for the islands of Elafonisos, the home of the mythical Cyclops as well as the site of magnificent beaches, and Kythira, the island where once stood a famous sanctuary to Aphrodite. Our own connection to Vatika came through Connie. She had a house in Neapoli along with a very large extended family there. They seemed to make up half the population as Connie was constantly pointing out one relative after another.

While Vatika didn't offer any major ruins or historical landmarks ("None of its manmade attractions are particularly compelling," said one guidebook), it did allow us to let our hair down, to relax into the life of a simpler part of Greece. For me, the transparent sea and the tangible feeling of ancient myths exuding from the land itself imbued a magical quality to our stay. It was as if the Muses had opened up our psyches, letting our personal odysseys unfold, often onto the pages of our writing. When we read our works-in-progress aloud, I could see that Vatika was transforming each of us in subtle and indelible ways.

Sometimes the changes actually happened right before our eyes. We watched with delight two very proper ladies, Doreen and Catherine, swing an ax at lifelong inhibitions as they stripped down to their underwear on a public beach. Catherine forced herself to eat octopus for the first time and tried out a few sexy tango steps with Virginia, our resident ballroom dancer. Doreen underwent a dramatic awakening after a phone conversation with one of her children. One sensed impending doom for the status quo at home.

But perhaps the most salient change that occurred was with our toilet problem. As we became more settled over the ensuing days, that mini-trashcan began to recede into the background of our concerns. Nobody went home early. There were no more backed-up systems. Ann was no longer "avoiding the whole question." Several women even mentioned how guilty they had begun to feel if they accidentally dropped paper into the toilet. Whereas at the beginning of our trip, we tended to avoid the public restrooms, by the end, everyone marveled at how much cleaner they were compared to American bathrooms. As for myself, I was happy to see my old sanguinity return. I no longer cringed at using the receptacle, though I never fell in love with it. I also noticed an unspoken etiquette for using it: clean side up, ALWAYS.

Greek for a Week

ANN KATHLEEN URE

℘

Yiorgos screeched to a halt in front of our Mesochori home and insisted that all five of us would easily fit into his taxi. He ushered four of my traveling companions into the back seat where—just like children—two sat forward and two sat back to share the space as best as possible. With rumps successfully planted aft, and mine in the front passenger seat, the taxi doors were slammed shut and off we went.

Our Greek and Yiorgos' English ran out of steam after a round of hellos. We settled into a polite, albeit brief, silence. Then Yiorgos switched on the radio and began to sing along.

"We're in Greece and we have a singing cab driver!" Catherine exclaimed. Each of us was enamored with anything Greek at that point in time. Every experience was new, fresh, memorable, and worthy of journaling. As his energy was contagious, soon all six heads in the taxi were bobbing in time to the spirited Greek music.

With his large, captive audience, and buoyed by our enthusiasm, Yiorgos increased his speed, weaving down the mountain and swaying to the beat. Then he lowered his window, extended his left arm, and began to snap his fingers. It was around the fourth or fifth curve that my travel mates in the backseat began to pale and nudge each other in alarm. They noticed, as I did, that Yiorgos' right hand was constantly adjusting the radio volume up while his left arm, fully extended into the evening breeze, kept time and, intermittently, encircled and caressed an unseen "air partner."

We nervously shot glances at one another, yet no one dared interrupt Yiorgos' process. Lord knows he didn't need another distraction. Eventually deposited, safely, at the foot of the mountain, we told our Greek hosts about our unusual, unnerving ride. They were not surprised, nor impressed, assuring us that many Greek cabbies used both hands to sing and dance while driving. What they did not explain, we recalled days later, was how they steered.

Throughout the week that followed, we Americans would soak up Greek culture with enthusiasm and abandon. However, adapting to Greek customs was a little trickier. It became clear that newcomers must learn the ropes. These are basic behaviors that, when mastered, provide travelers with the opportunity to experience Greece as an insider, also known as becoming Greek for a week.

In rural Greece, no one stops at stop signs. Apparently, they serve as suggestions only. On our long drive down the mountain from Monemvasia, I realized that our driver didn't even slow down for these occasional postings.

Picturing myself behind the wheel, and having already adapted to song-and-dance-man cabbies, I reflected that driving in Greece had a lot in common with driving in downtown Manhattan, or maneuvering a race car through a video game maze. The goal was to modulate between acceleration and deceleration to avoid oncoming obstacles without ever coming to a complete stop.

This became doubly exciting when it was performed with only one hand. Those drivers who were not dancing with their left hands were usually flipping Greek worry beads—that dangled from key chains—with their right hands. (No surprise there, given the absence of any rules of the road.) Rumor had it that one of the cabbies was so successful in avoiding complete stops that he hadn't had his brake pads replaced since the last appearance of Haley's comet in 1986. And, after having ridden with him, I'd wager that he had no plans to replace them again til its scheduled reappearance in 2062.

Naps are required. In Vatika, everything and everybody shuts down from three to six in the afternoon. As visitors, we too were expected to nap or at least disengage for this three-hour period. The rationale, we were told, was relief from the heat of the late afternoon. Regardless of the motivation, it helped explain how Greek days so easily roll over into Greek nights.

Time is more fluid there. Asked to prepare for a late afternoon workshop, we later learned that it would take place at seven o'clock.

In my world, seven is early evening: my work is done; I've got a glass of wine in front of me; and, if it's winter and I've no other plans, I may have even have slipped into my flannel pajamas and robe for the evening. Here, we slipped into pajamas and gabbed into the evening too. But our Greek pajama party began at midnight when our host donned her nightgown and four-inch heels to conduct tango lessons. And this on a "school night!"

The extended days usually meant that the following mornings would begin no earlier than nine with a leisurely, light breakfast and a much later, and heartier, lunch. Adapting to this new regimen, and I use that word loosely, produced spectacular results. Witness the beastly hot day when we were dropped off for four hours to shop and have lunch in Neapoli. Four hours? I couldn't imagine spending more than an hour walking the hot and dusty streets to look at tourist fare. My friends agreed, so we took sixty minutes to pick up gifts for home, then headed to an outdoor café where we spent the next three hours decompressing under an umbrella. There commenced a leisurely family-style lunch, sampling Greek salad, fried calamari, garlic and clam pasta, our first Greek pizza, and lemonade. We talked. We traded stories. The tables around us were full with others who had also escaped the heat and were kicked back in conversation with beer, wine and no other plans other than to enjoy the meal and their company. Now that's civilized.

Be prepared to join a Greek twelve-step program. As opposed to such programs at home that require abstinence and anonymity, these classes were held at night on a large patio, under the stars, and with a full complement of alcoholic beverages. Our classes were taught by young ladies, the sisters Alexa and Chrysa, who coaxed us out of our chairs with promises of inclusion and tension-reduction. As Chrysa took one hand and Alexa the other, I prepared myself for an intervention. Instead, I was launched into my first Greek dancing lesson.

"Come on, join us!" Alexa appealed to the others. "It's easy. You just have to count to twelve!" Oh, were it only that easy.

"It's all about the two, four and eight counts," Chrysa cheerfully instructed us. "Lead with your right foot on one, step behind with your left on two, step side, cross in front on four, step side on five, six, seven, rock front on eight, step in place for nine and ten, back for eleven, in place for twelve and then lead off again with the right foot to begin again."

We danced in a circle with arms interlocked, though it was a rare bit of magic to find us all on the same foot and moving in the same direction at any one time. Like karaoke, this was definitely an activity that was more fun to do than it was to observe. While watching, I found myself grimacing at others' missteps and wondering if the white man's disease (an inability to find the beat) had rubbed off on them. But everyone slowly improved, including me, though I did utter countless numbers of "damns" when, at the eighth count, my left foot rocked backward instead of forward.

With Chrysa's unwavering vocalization of the twelve-step count, I experienced moments of getting it right and some swan-like fluidity in my movements. She earned an A-plus for her patience and teaching skills. But it was her sister Alexa whose dancing stood out. In fact, it was exquisite. Young and strong, and with long coltish legs, her feet were so light that she barely skimmed the surface of our dance floor. While demonstrating a second dance that we newcomers could only stand back and admire, she awed us with her elegance. A gesture as brief and simple as raising her left foot off the ground at a slight angle for a half beat was inexplicably lovely. We could have watched her for hours under those stars.

Listen with your eyes. "It's Greek to me" is one of the truest truisms ever uttered, as it is near impossible to comprehend the spoken or written word while in Greece. I marveled at our group's concerted efforts to snatch a bit of meaning here or there while listening to conversations. Each time we were in the presence of natives, we were quiet and attentive, heads tilted slightly to the right in that posture associated with dogs who are straining to interpret humans' senseless babble.

Understanding words on street signs, maps, store shelves, and product labels was even more useless. It was further complicated by the Greeks use of two alphabets: the classic and the modern. This meant that the same indecipherable word would often be depicted with multiple spellings.

The Greeks amazing appetite for speaking loudly, gesticulating and showing physical affection seemed to be their way of compensating for a language that is understood by few. It was this expressiveness and body language that enabled us to interpret a bit of what was going on around us. For example, when greeted with a bear hug and double kisses (left and right cheeks) we could be fairly confident that we were welcome. Similarly, the singing and dancing of our Greek dinner companions in restaurants, and between courses, was a clear sign that the evening was progressing well.

I imagined how difficult it would be to understand anything spoken by our new friends had they possessed the limited flair of the British. A Greek conversation—delivered with such polite, buttoned-up behavior and mannerisms—would baffle even the most sensitive observers. On this point, all of us Americans agreed. Without the body language and effusiveness we'd come to depend upon, a young man taking up a woman's hand to propose marriage could as easily have been interpreted as a citizen's arrest.

Octopus and ouzo is a complete meal. This concept, coupled with the fact that we were to dine at the establishment famous for this limited menu, was a cause of distress for one or two of my travel mates. The anise-flavored liquor, alone, was a turn-off for some. They had no intention of trying ouzo and were not the least bit fascinated by how its clear color turned opaque with the addition of water or ice.

In particular, Catherine, a fellow writer, had announced, even before the trip began, that she would not be seduced into sampling either of the 'O' foods. This became a call-to-action for me and some of the others who thought that a trip half way round the world presented the perfect opportunity to take a few risks, try something new.

At the first possible opportunity we took Catherine to the octopus and ouzo outdoor bar for an afternoon snack. Glasses of water and charming individual bottles of ouzo were ordered by our Greek accomplice. Then they were served, all around, so that she wasn't given a chance to say no. Getting Catherine to try the ouzo wasn't that difficult. She wasn't a teetotaler, and she liked licorice, so she took a sip and said it was "Okay." It was a measured response. She likely, and correctly, assumed that the ouzo wasn't the only new experience we had in store for her that afternoon.

The octopus had also been ordered in Greek and it arrived on small appetizer plates a few minutes later. Grilled and thinly sliced, it didn't look at all like an eight-legged, ink-squirting, sucker-covered sea monster. Still, Catherine demurred. And a full-court press by her table mates ensued. I was among the pushiest, I'm sure, taking on the role of a paid coach who has led a shy would-be skydiver to the door of the plane to encourage her to jump.

"This is all about personal growth!" I cajoled. "We didn't really come here to write; we came to l-i-v-e!" It sounded a bit desperate and misguided since our focus was just a small piece of cooked fish. Still, Catherine shook her head, suggesting that her personal growth could be deferred for at least one more day.

Switching tactics, we collectively eased off and opted to try the octopus ourselves. It was surprisingly tasty.

"Catherine!" I began again, with enthusiasm. "It tastes like chicken!" With that innocuous but true statement, her resolve melted. And so Catherine took her first bite of grilled octopus. We all celebrated her achievement with clinks of our glasses, cries of "*Yamas!*" and small sips of ouzo. Except for Catherine. She took a huge gulp, the ouzo having become the lesser of two evils at her disposal. And the next day, to her chagrin, we got her to eat her first grilled mussel too.

You can't take it with you. Returning to the United States and to my own routine, I made every effort to sustain what I learned and loved about Greek people and their customs. Sadly, some things just wouldn't translate. I shivered in the white gauzy shirts and slacks, so apropos to Vatika, when our summer fog failed to lift til noon, then rolled back in before five. I gave up on the leisurely lunches I'd become accustomed to when friends couldn't make the time, reminding me that this was the land of gulp and run. So, once again, I've begun to eat at my desk, alone.

When I attempted to dance while driving on Highway 101 South I nearly lost my left arm to a speeding Subaru. And my boss just glared at me when I mentioned that I'd lately become accustomed to three-hour naps. Worst of all was my failed attempt to demonstrate Greek dancing to my family. I knew things had deteriorated badly when they pointed out that my routine didn't add up. I was two steps shy of twelve.

And so, despite my best efforts, I've learned that you really can't take it with you. But the memories are strong, the new friendships are true, and there are always pictures to remind me of any details I may have forgotten. With or without the daily observance of customs odd and dear, I know that I really was Greek for a week. And I can always go back.

My Greek Ancestors

M.J. PRAMIK (A.K.A. M.J. PRAMIKOMEOSIS)

ᕀ

I am the only Greek in my family.

The fishing net draped across the front entry adds a definitive new leitmotif to my San Francisco Edwardian home. The building has a blue-tinged white luster much like the structures that cling to the angular precipices of Greece's southern Peloponnese area of Lakonia. According to Greek lore, the fishing net, having survived the washings of forty different currents, is so pure and clear it will bless my home and guard against evil. You see, I've just returned from Greece and have discovered my true Greek ancestry.

The charm against the *Mati*, the Evil Eye, now dangles on my rearview mirror as I speed along California's highways. The Greeks believe this talisman protects a person from another's bad vibes or harmful thoughts. I have obliged each of my daughters to wear the deep blue "evil-eye" charm, and have secretly pinned one inside my son's drumstick bag as well. He attends music school in New York City soon and, goddess knows, he'll need it there.

My family's official genealogy records that each of my four grandparents emigrated from Poland to America's port of entry, Ellis Island, where their names are clearly chiseled on the stone tablets that demark the island's perimeter. Cousins have produced an official photographed copy of Grandpa Pramik's signature on the entry legend, when Poland was occupied by Austria. However, I have often suspected that I was adopted. The childhood fable, "The Ugly Duckling," had a deep resonance for me during my tender years.

My sojourn in the Peloponnese clarified how growing up in a Polish, Czech, and Italian hamlet in Ohio prepared me for my Greek life. Cabbage rolls look a lot like *dolmades*. My mother made great summer salads. She chopped cucumbers and onions adding oil and vinegar for the vegetables to swim in. Virginia (Vir-gee-NEE-ah to her Greek compatriots)—our host for the Vatika workshop—mirrored my mother in her cooking. Greek dishes flowed from her tiny stove. The kitchen, compact and complete, resembled the galley of a ship, taut with stored white café dinner wear and authentic antique pottery. I searched everywhere with my eyes but could not see where she stowed the food supplies that would appear on her table for the next meal. My mother cooked like this, always preparing twice as much food as was needed. Just in case. In case more people appeared at the door, such as the family member who brought the other cousins who just happened to be in town. The Polish tradition of setting a place at the table for those family members who had died had taught me to always set an extra place.

Here, as we faced Neapolis Bay and the Aegean Sea beyond, a staple of nearly every meal is the Greek salad. Not the usurper we have in the United States, but the veritable Greek *choriatiko* salad composed of luscious vine-picked tomatoes, slivers of Vatika's sweetest red onions, slices of cucumber and black Kalamata olives, delivered with a thick slice of the whitest succulent feta dusted with Mediterranean spices and drizzled with olive oil. Finally, a blessing of lemon juice is sprinkled over the riotous mound of colorful vegetables.

Noodles were another part of my upbringing. *Halushkie*, a blend of flat pasta, cabbage, butter, and onions sautéed to perfection readied me for Virginia's noodles and cheese casseroles. My grandmother baked cheese pies with a touch of sweetness while Virginia, our Greek mother for the week, crafted cheese pies that hosted a savory tanginess and zest I hope to soon emulate in my San Francisco kitchen. One evening, at a wine tasting featuring local Vatistas wines, we were treated to a meat platter that held sliced sausage, much like the Polish *kielbasa*, and *keftedakia*, much akin to meatballs. However, liquid refreshments on the southern peninsula varied from the Polish thirst quenchers. In Vatika, we were treated to excellent deep red Monemvasia regional *krasi* (wine), rather than the traditional Eastern European whiskey shot with a beer chaser.

In Virginia's kitchen and at her table, I ate without stopping, those second helpings tasting even better than the first. All the Greek dishes laden with vegetables whispered so "wholesome," "natural," and "light," because they were made with the secret ingredient of love.

Virginia always set the table with a Grecian blue tablecloth. Breakfast included thick Greek yogurt squeezed to a consistency of pudding and laced with honey from the countryside and jams reminiscent of the berry jams of my childhood. The same blue cloth hosted a lunch of the obligatory Greek salad and a basket of sliced bread; cheese pie, *tiropita*, with its flaky filo; noodles and cheese; aubergine with a filling of hard cheese baked with tomatoes and herbs. Some days a fish dish would appear. Other meals were vegetarian fare that overwhelmed the palate and sated the soul as well as the body. I had no problem adapting to this diet.

In Greece, mothering is part of the psyche as well. Gracious, attractive, svelte, stylish, able to wear a white sarong in a multitude of knots and ties, Virginia quite magically prepared dinners and "light" lunches that carried us through the afternoon, all the while serenading us with Greek folk songs of love and Piaf-esque ballads and minding her children in Athens. Virginia, kissing all on one cheek and then the other, was our earth mother, the all-accepting mother I always wished I had.

Hugs and *filakia* (a.k.a. kisses) are the Greek greetings among men and women. For those of us caught in the sanitized computer age, this ritual can take a bit of getting used to. Kissing both cheeks and hugging as a greeting was performed by all. Several times our taxi driver would hop out and joyously greet a neighbor while we waited and watched. I had always longed for that human touch. American life can feel empty with its "ships passing in the night" existence. I knew I was Greek because these boisterous greetings and energetic kisses felt so natural.

I have always used my hands when speaking. My own mother once asked if I was Mediterranean, focusing on the Italian love for hand gestures. She should know, I thought, when I was old enough to question authority (age five). Her query was my first inkling that I was different, an ugly Mediterranean duckling floating in the wrong Ohio pond.

Then last year I met *agapi moo* Connie, one of our hosts for this summer's Greek revelry, on a journey in France. Her hand pirouettes quadrupled mine. I had found a kindred spirit! One who bestowed a welcome on both cheeks, while speaking volumes with her hands.

In Greece, I could use my hands without embarrassment. Like the wide flapping of a swan, I need not shy away from flamboyant circles. Watching Connie diagram the air, messages arced across the atmosphere. Fingers declared, "I'll see you at four o'clock precisely." Taxi drivers, when not crossing themselves, would drive with their left arm dangling out the window and wave minute textual greetings to fellow drivers or pedestrians in passing. The palm facing inward culling of the air sends a goodbye between Greeks. An outward facing palm with five fingers splayed was not a good idea, as the inhabitants consider this a rude gesture. No wonder taxis did not stop for the five American goddesses using standard New Yorkese for "Taxi, please."

Another Greek inherited trait, GMT, or Greek Maybe Time, operates as a genuine center of my biological clock. My children can attest to this evidence of my Greek ancestry. They often grew impatient with my, "I'll be right there." Responses to their pleas for attention would some days take hours. Now I realize that the abundance of unfinished projects decorating my home parrot the multitudinous unfinished houses that pock the Greek landscape. Hulks of rebar and dark gray concrete, these shrines to GMT heartened my views. Rather than dampen the vistas, they spoke to me, "Ah, life is so full, so little time to do everything."

After spending nearly two weeks in Greece in the hillside village of Mesochori on the southern most point of the Peloponnese, I am certain of my Greek roots. Little do my children realize I have begun their dowries. Greek parents buy each daughter a house upon marriage; I may have to bend a little on this one as my son would feel slighted. Although law canceled the dowry, *prika*, in 1983, parents still bestow refrigerators and beds, and sometimes houses on their female offspring. With today's California housing prices, I may have to attenuate this long-held custom. Perhaps I could buy each child one of the myriad of unfinished homes that languish in the villages of Lakonia, next to hotels or across vacant lots in Athens, adjacent to glorious classical buildings.

Upon my return from the Peloponnese, I prepared meals resembling Virginia's. Greek spices infused my cook's psyche. California vine-ripened tomatoes and crunchy cucumbers in season in mid-July created a *real* Greek salad. As I served my brother a Sunday meal in my newly-inspired goddess persona, he quipped "How long is this Greek phase going to last?" He'll rue the day he said that, he of the only *blue* eyes in our Ohio Polish family. My son, however, seems taken with the *baklava* and chunks of sweet melon swimming in native juices served with every dinner. My slicing and arranging the red and light green fruit on the plate seems to bless the flavors a hundredfold, just as Virginia's hands did in Mesochori.

Henry Miller in *The Colossus of Maroussi* observed, "For a Greek every event, no matter how stale, is always unique. He is always doing the same thing for the first time...." Living in Greece for nearly two weeks set my Greek DNA vibrating.

Dancing on Connie's patio in Neapoli on a balmy July evening awaiting the full moon, brought back a flood of memories of customary Polish weddings celebrated nearly every weekend in my Ohio hamlet. Connie's American-born nieces counted out the steps to the traditional *hasapikos*, one-two, cross over, three and four, five, six, seven, eight. The intensity of their tutelage and the preciseness of the count could not counter the effect of the magical essence of the local wines. Inhaling the night, I stopped counting the steps after several dances and gave in to my inner Greek. Just sway with the music, my genetic memory counseled. *Opah!* Ah, then my steps flowed. My hips swayed under my white tulle skirt and the night air picked up my steps. Around we twirled, circled. I caught sight of Orion's belt in the dark sky. I had begun to glide like a graceful swan across the stone floor, no longer awkward or foreign.

Living among this welcoming people, I experienced *parea*—the Greek word for belonging to the human community. A swan among swans, let's say. Today's Greeks welcome all into their community. It's a palpable, intensely real emotion.

Although Ellis Island registers my grandparents as Polish, perhaps they honeymooned in Greece a century ago. In the past, ancestors were known to have traveled far and wide. After two weeks among the oregano and thyme and the incessant cicadas and promising figs, I am convinced that I am Greek. My heart tells me so.

From Vatika Kitchens

BARBARA J. EUSER

$\curlyvee$

"I myself feel that there is nothing more delightful than when the festive mood reigns in the hearts of all the people and the banqueters listen to a minstrel from their seats in the hall, while the tables before them are laden with bread and meat, and a steward carries round the wine he has drawn from the bowl and fills their cups. This, to my way of thinking, is perfection."
— HOMER, *THE ODYSSEY*

The Municipality of Vatika comprises the town of Neapoli and fourteen villages in the surrounding area. Village tavernas offer ample opportunity to sample regional cuisine. In the village of Lachi, Matina Economou owns and operates the *Taverna Oenopylos*

(The Wine Jug), otherwise known by her nickname, *Matoula's*. In the village of Faraklo, Panayiotis Billinis runs the mountainside taverna *El Faraklo*.

To add authentic local flavor to this collection of essays, we asked Matoula and Panayiotis for recipes for some of our favorite dishes. Vatika gardens produce tomatoes, onions, peppers, eggplants, zucchini, potatoes and other vegetables in abundance. Matoula and Panayiotis are known for their creative use of local produce. Matoula gave us her recipes for Stuffed Zucchini Flowers, Long Green Peppers Stuffed with Feta Cheese, and Eggplants with Feta Cheese. Panayiotis gave us his recipes for Kaponata, Potatoes Saganaki, and Salata tis Trellis.

STUFFED ZUCCHINI FLOWERS

Ingredients

25 zucchini flowers
1 cup of rice
2 grated tomatoes
1 grated onion
Fennel, parsley, dill
½ teaspoon salt
Fresh ground pepper
2 tablespoons olive oil

Δ Wash the flowers and cut their stems.

Δ Mix the rest of the ingredients together in a bowl.

Δ Fill the buds with about a teaspoon of the mix and fold the petals on top. Don't overfill, as the rice will expand.

Δ Place them in a pan one next to the other. Pour on olive oil and sprinkle with salt.

Δ Cover them with a plate (so that they don't fall apart while simmering).

Δ Add a glass of water and simmer for about 20 minutes.

LONG GREEN PEPPERS STUFFED WITH FETA CHEESE

Ingredients

8 long, mild green peppers
¼ cup of olive oil
I grated onion
2 tomatoes cut in small pieces
I tablespoon of ketchup
Pepper, oregano, a bit of cayenne pepper
Parsley
½ pound feta cheese cut in big chunks
Do not add any salt because feta cheese is salty

Δ Wash the peppers and remove the seeds and stems.

Δ Cut the tops of the peppers to create 'lids.'

Δ Boil the peppers for 5 minutes.

Δ Remove them from water and let them cool.

Δ In a frying pan, fry the onion in the oil. Add tomato, ketchup, pepper and oregano. Stir for a while and then remove from the heat.

Δ Let the filling cool a bit and then add the feta cheese and the parsley.

Δ Fill the peppers and close them with the 'lids.'

Δ Either coat the stuffed peppers with oil and put them on the grill, or put them in the oven and bake at medium temperature (325° F) for 20 minutes.

EGGPLANTS WITH FETA CHEESE

Ingredients

6 large eggplants
1 lb. feta cheese
2 lbs. ripe tomatoes
1 tablespoon tomato puree
Fresh ground pepper
1 sliced onion
2-3 cloves of garlic
1 hot red pepper, finely chopped
1 long mild green pepper, finely chopped
¼ cup of olive oil

Δ Wash and cut the eggplants in thin slices. Put them in a bowl of water and salt and let them soak for an hour to take the bitterness away.

Δ In a frying pan pour the oil, add the onion, the garlic, and the peppers. Fry well and add the tomatoes, the tomato puree, the pepper, and the parsley. Simmer.

Δ Rinse the eggplant slices and pat dry.

Δ Fry the eggplant slices in plenty of oil, then place them on absorbent paper towels.

Δ Cut the feta cheese in long wands.

Δ Wrap each slice of eggplant around a piece of feta cheese.

Δ Place the eggplant/feta rolls in a pan and pour the sauce on top.

Δ Bake in a preheated oven at 350° F for 20 minutes.

KAPONATA

Ingredients

6 bell peppers
2 large eggplants
6 tomatoes
I large onion
I teaspoon sugar
I tablespoon honey
I tablespoon capers
12 green seedless olives, sliced
Olive oil for frying

- Δ Clean peppers and cut into large squares
- Δ Slice eggplant, salt it, after one-half hour rinse and pat dry
- Δ Lightly fry peppers, then eggplant
- Δ Sauté chopped onion

To make sauce, cook together:

- Δ Seeded, chopped tomatoes
- Δ Sauted onion
- Δ Sugar

At the end, add honey, capers, and sliced green seedless olives.
In a glass dish, spread out a layer of eggplant covered with a layer
of peppers.
Cover with the sauce and refrigerate two days.
Serve with yogurt and/or feta cheese.

POTATOES SAGANAKI

Ingredients

3 potatoes, baked, then sliced
7 pieces dried tomato
4 oz. Roquefort cheese
Fresh, crushed ginger
Coriander
Olive oil to coat casserole
Salt
3 oz. grated Parmesan cheese

Δ In a shallow casserole, place olive oil and broken chunks of Roquefort cheese.

Δ Arrange pieces of dried tomato in a layer in casserole.

Δ Cover with a thick layer of sliced, baked potatoes.

Δ Sprinkle with fresh, crushed ginger and a touch of coriander and salt.

Δ Sprinkle Parmesan cheese on top, heat in oven until Parmesan melts.

SALATA TIS TRELLIS

Ingredients

4 finely chopped tomatoes
5 finely grated carrots
1 finely diced onion
1 can pinto beans, drained and rinsed
1 can corn, drained and rinsed
3 cooked beets (run through blender)
Juice of one lemon
Balsamic vinegar to taste
Salt to taste

Δ Toss ingredients together in a large salad bowl. Serve chilled.

A Place in the Heart

C.K. MᴄFᴇʀʀɪɴ

⟩⟨

I did not know where Neapoli was; even Greece's exact location in the Mediterranean was a bit of a mystery to me. In my earlier travels through Europe, it had been a goal to visit Greece. But it never happened. Now, twenty years later, angst grew as my departure date approached. I was leaving for Greece to meet and travel with a group of creative women writers. In the travel section of my local bookstore, I briefly picked up a book and browsed a map of Greece looking for the areas I planned to visit: Athens—found it. Piraeus—yes, just outside Athens. Meso . . . hmmm. I couldn't remember the name of the town we planned to stay in. Meso-something. I knew we were going south. I followed the southern outline of the continent looking at all the names that began with "M." I didn't find it. I left the store without a map of Greece.

My fears were realized even before I left California. My flight from San Francisco was delayed three hours due to mechanical difficulties. There was no way to make up the time. I missed my connecting flight in Amsterdam. I began to wonder if I'd ever make it to Greece. After ten hours in Amsterdam and two days of travel, I finally arrived in Athens in the middle of the night. An IKEA sign glowed on the ground below us as the plane lowered onto the runway. It made me feel confused, like I'd never left the United States.

Taxis were lined up along the curb. I was very grateful I did not have to hunt for one. It was just at that moment that I realized I really did not know where I was going! I thought to myself, "Do I have the address? How could I be so unprepared?" A wave of panic seized me. I walked up to one of the drivers.

"I need to go here. Can you help me to get to this place?" I pushed a printed page of paper, with directions in Greek, under the driver's nose. Our host, Connie Burke, expatriate extraordinaire, whose grandparents came from Greece and who lives here most of the year, had emailed everyone the directions to her home in Pasalimani, Piraeus, about an hour south of Athens. The driver nodded and put my red suitcase in the trunk. He would take me. I did not know any Greek. I couldn't phonetically sound out any road signs. I was no help to him. The best thing I could do was be quiet and let him read the note in Greek, which I did. He read slowly, his fingers following along each word. He read the note again with his fingers as if the message had been in braille. Maybe he couldn't read. That thought did cross my mind. The next thing I knew, we were off. I was at the mercy of Hermes, god of travel. "May he get me there safely," I said to myself. At the first opportunity I was going to buy a map.

Shifting in the seat for a better view—up, back, leaning over— I observed a culture that appeared to be in transition: old stone buildings, white, run-down, abandoned, often covered with graffiti; auto row businesses; a new subway that looked barely used; a four-lane freeway. I searched the surroundings trying to orient myself in this unfamiliar place. Finally, without success, I sat back, let out an audible sigh, and let the unfamiliar scenery wash over me.

"I get you there. Just sleep," said my gentle guide. He was an older man, with a bit of a slouch, who squinted when concentrating. He drove the only non-Mercedes car in the row of airport taxis. Our eyes met in the rearview mirror. I relaxed. The last memory I had was of the warm wind from the open window caressing my face.

What seemed like only minutes later I heard, "O.K., here." I sat up, refocused and looked blankly into the dark. He was pointing to a building.

"O.K., wait," I said as I used my hands to gesture for him to stop, don't run off, don't leave me behind. "I want to be sure," I murmured, as I hopped out of the car, ran over to the building, checked the address and rang the doorbell.

In a short time, I heard sleepy, quiet steps. The latch of the tall entry doors un-clicked and echoed down the street. The door opened and there stood Linda, one of two writing instructors and my dearest friend, her long, shiny black hair pulled back, looking sleepy and worried. I have known Linda longer than anyone outside my immediate family. I met her when I was cresting adolescence and yearned for the guidance and example of a big sister. She came into my life as my brother's girlfriend. It has been a love affair ever since. We looked at each other, wrapped one another in a warm embrace and cried out, "Yeah!" I turned to the cab driver, ran down the stairs and thanked him, clapping in his honor.

"Shhh, shhh," he cried out, smiling, and pointing to the neighbors so as not to wake them up. I grabbed my bags, paid him, plus a thank you tip, and began the next leg of my journey.

We had only a day in Athens before traveling by motor coach to our final destination. With that in mind, a few of us headed out early the next morning to the Acropolis. We were five women and finally flagged down a taxi driver who informed us it was against the law for taxis to take five people. We quickly flagged down a second taxi and headed for the base of the Acropolis. I had to get a map. I was without reference to anything around me and couldn't stand it. It felt horribly disorienting.

In my earlier travel days, I took great pride in my ability to orient myself to a place. Arriving in a new city, town, or village, usually by train, backpack in tow, the first thing I would do was get a map of the area. Putting my pack in a locker, I would spend the first hour or two just walking the city like an animal exploring its territory. I felt the need to recognize a few streets, check out the cafes, have a beer and a bite.

At the kiosk on the walk up to purchase tickets to the Acropolis, there were all kinds of maps. I bought an Athens street map in English which I thought would help me in the short term. But it was difficult to use as the street signs were in Greek. Instead, we explored the narrow streets of the surrounding Plaka following our own intuition. Linda had purchased a map as well, her choice being wiser: a large and detailed Michelin map of the entire country. I flashed back to the many times in my life when Linda's wisdom has guided me, shedding light on a dark path, helping me from one point to another. I smiled at the thought. Her map served as a reference as we traveled south.

The next morning, packed and ready, the whole group—now eleven—loaded the bus and embarked on the journey that would take us to the southern Peloponnese. For the first time, I was traveling in a group instead of alone. Not unwilling, but apprehensive, my earlier travel memories encroached, standing in the aisle, like an extra member on the bus with no seat. George, our professional driver, tall, Greek, with a middle-aged belly and dark mustache, was friendly to all, but barked out directions as necessary to round us up and move us out. As we departed the city, he maneuvered the narrow streets with care while the locals stared. I imagined them betting as to whether or not he might hit a parked car. The odds were good.

I still did not have my own map of Greece. I had learned, however, that Neapoli was on the southern coast of the Peloponnese in the region called Vatika which overlooked the Aegean Sea, a place full of myths, legends and lore.

Chatter, song, and excitement among mostly strangers filled a good part of our five-hour drive. Some wrote in journals. Others dozed as the sun peeked in and out from behind the clouds. My eyes darted to capture each homestead, hillside and seaside view. I felt frustrated as the varied countryside whizzed by.

"Linda, may I borrow your map?" I could at least try to find where we were on the road.

Linda dug around and handed me the Michelin map. I opened it up and began reviewing. Again, it wasn't so easy to locate myself as the road signs were in Greek. I was able to find Neapoli along the coast but not our final destination, Mesochori, the village in which we were staying. Nor did I find any reference to Vatika. We passed over the amazing and historic Isthmus of Corinth with its deep channel and steep sheer walls. Imagining myself as the water in the channel, I wrote:

I watch you watching me as my colors dance with the changing light.
In morning's dawn I am deep blue, blue like black, lacking prisms' light,
Quietly dense as I carry you to commerce.
At high midday I've churned. Light is harsh.
I'm paler now—blue like Alaska, ice-blue, white-blue, polluted with bleach.
I'm harsh and tired of your modern travels.
The night is mine, no matter your need. I'm cool and quiet, sleek and black,
Save for the sprinkle of moonlight washing against my channeled walls.

I managed to find our lunch stop on the map, the ancient city of Sparta, the capital of Lakonia, two hours from our southern home. It was hot. I wanted to sit and take in the town, watch the light change, the locals walk by. But we had a schedule to keep. We finished lunch and re-boarded the bus. The map didn't mean much at this point, so I put it away.

The window was my portal, and I was absorbed by the hillsides—dry, craggy and mysterious; blue water under clouds that changed from white to dark grey against the mountain slopes. Crumbled Byzantine castles stood upon hilltops, ancient and abandoned. I wanted to move slowly through this very different place. I wanted to dig my heels into the earth and scream, "Stop!" I needed to feel the dirt between my fingers, touch the old world, its secrets, history, held in the shadow of the clouds. I felt the stories of old wash over me—ancient ways I seemed to remember: lives lost in battles, pain, pride, knowledge rising, like these mountains, showing the way.

Our bus made its way down the mountain range and we finally entered Neapoli, the late afternoon sun still high and strong. A coastal village, Neapoli was white against blue waters and color-dappled hillsides. But we didn't stop. We wound around and headed up a mountain, slow going on a switchbacked road, pavement giving way to dirt, to finally arrive in the hillside village of Mesochori. My body had arrived; my mind had yet to catch up. I had no connection to this place.

"Linda, do you mind if I keep the map for awhile?" I asked. "I want to look up some things."

"No problem," she replied.

From any spot in Mesochori, the views are breathtaking,

whether looking back down the mountain past Neapoli out to the Aegean Sea or up over the hillsides to the mountain ranges. I could never have imagined a place like this. It is so high up that the coastline can be viewed for miles beyond Neapoli. White-domed churches dot the landscape with their crosses on top like candles on a buttercream cake. Mesochori looks more like a little neighborhood than a village. Even strangers are greeted as they pass. I discovered many of the neighbors had family roots here, but had lived in Canada or Australia or South Africa, only to return for the peace that is found here, for the beauty. Others never left this little village, their creviced faces holding stories I could only feel as I looked into their eyes.

One day, still confused about our place with this new-old world, I pulled one of my fellow writers aside.

"Chrysa, could I ask you a few questions?" I inquired.

"Sure!" she replied, open and willing. Chrysa is Greek-American and has been coming to this area all of her twenty years. Her *theia*, or aunt, is Connie, our Greek-American organizer. Their family has many relatives in Neapoli. Chrysa and her sister, Alexa, are both beautiful, intelligent young women, who attended our workshop and contributed much to our experience. They taught us how to Greek dance, helped us with taxis, told stories of the "evil eye" and much more. I pulled out Linda's map, opened it up and had a geography lesson with Chrysa. The Peloponnese, I discovered, is shaped like a paw, with four claws that extend out. The Prefecture of Lakonia takes up the better half of two of the middle claws. Neapoli sits right on the coast in Neapolis Bay in the region of Vatika, within Lakonia. Mesochori, sits high on its perch above Neapoli. The lesson continued and the doors to the region opened a crack.

A few days later, on a ferry to the island of Elafonisos, I began to understand the people who make up this part of Greece. Through Virginia, our radiant host, I met Captain Vassilis, a modern Poseidon, god of the sea. Like a gull free to fly from one harbor to another, so sails Captain Vassilis. He reads the *meltemi*, the wind that churns the waters of Neapolis Bay. Behind sun-streaked eyes, he understands the changing currents and tides. His life is his boats on the water: the *Agonistis* and the *Vassilis Papoulis*. Weighted like an anchor, he barks commands across the hull. His earthy legs, brown like a mulberry trunk, ride the boat as a surfer's—sure, balanced. But to know him is to see him among friends, his smile wide and mischievous. Generous of heart, just ask him your favor. His specialty is song. On his own or in duet, out loud or under his breath, while he enjoys his food, he sings. He sings the old songs of love, the songs of Neapolis Bay. It was through his eyes, the songs he and Virginia sang together and their dancing, that I began to understand this area, the people, and to feel a sense of place.

Looking out from the narrow balcony of my room, I take in the arid landscape, the colors, sounds and the feeling of this paradise. My mind wanders from person to person through the days filled with new sites and experiences. My heart is overwhelmed with a new understanding for the people who opened their homes, hearts, voices and music to us. I have Linda's map, but it is not the map I need. The connection with the people, their land, their stories and songs are the real map and my guide to understanding. At last, I have found a sense of place in Neapolis Bay. It is a place in the heart.

In Vatika

Linda Watanabe McFerrin

ﻉ

Vessels take shelter in Neapolis Bay. The shallow crescent of safety is a refuge from the shipwrecking winds of Cape Maleas and the stormy seas that tear around the first bony knuckle of that rocky fist of land known as the Peloponnese. It is early July and all around us the *meltemi* roars, sweeps through villages and rooms, ruffling through things long settled, stirring memories and emotions, disturbing dreams. I stand on one of the many terraces of the whitewashed eyrie that is Virginia's home, looking down on a rocky, herb-colored landscape dotted with olive trees and crossed by long, cinnamon ribbons of road. We are here to write about a region unfamiliar even to many Greeks, though some of them know it as Vies, a rural municipality located at land's end in the Prefecture of Lakonia. When I mention my destination to a Greek friend in Athens, he is mystified. "Where in the world is Vatika?" he writes. And I am surprised.

Where is it? It is south, south, south—on that knob of a peninsula that is distinguished by destinations with more recognizable names: Neapoli, Monemvasia, Elafonisos. It is the point at which the Aegean and Ionian Seas kiss in a dangerous union that wrecks ships and ruins sailors. It was here that the treacherous winds of Cape Maleas blew Odysseus off course, impeding his return to his Ionian kingdom after the long Trojan Wars, sending him off on another ten years of hard travel. Legend has it that Paris and Helen took shelter in the sanctuary of Athena that once rose on the island of Elafonisos. This part of Greece is a place where, like the boats floating patiently on the water below, I took refuge several years ago after my father's death and at the outset of my mother's slow descent into Alzheimers. I found a safe harbor in Neapoli where the light sluices down the chalk-colored walls in a peachy dribble at sunset; where the cats drowse on balconies or on the well-swept walkways beside seaside tavernas; where large pea-green grasshoppers sit and stare at you from the sun-drenched steps of a blue-domed church or cling to your clothing with jagged legs, a look of pacifist understanding in their ruby-red eyes. It is a place where my dear friend Connie has a home that has held me in the past, a bed that witnessed my nightmares.

This time teaching brings me here: the chance to work again with a talented group of women writers. We will comb the surroundings for stories. But something else is churned up by the pervasive winds. I find myself floundering upon the rocks of my worst fears and my darkest memories. We are deep in mythic territory. Neapoli is said to have been founded by one of the sons of Heracles, the Greek hero and demigod, child of Zeus and Alcmene. The island of Kythira, to the south, is thought to be the birthplace of Aphrodite, goddess of love. In the waters around Elafonisos are chamber tombs from the prehistoric period and, with them, an entire prehistoric town buried beneath the sea. It was on Elafonisos that Kinadis, captain of the Mycenaean king Menelaus' ship, was purportedly interred. I think of the tales of gods and goddesses, of Athens and Lakonia, of the powerful Mycenaean kings, of Agamemnon and Menelaus, of Achilles and Odysseus, and I am lost in them. Greece always catches me up, dashes me against the rocks, finds me again.

My first trip to Greece was years ago with my husband, Lawrence. We were traveling around Europe after the death of our newborn daughter, Marissa, our only child. We came towing regret, weighted with sorrow. We came running. Germany, France—we tried to escape the bitter specter of Marissa's mortality and ours. But the world, as we saw it, was grainy and gray, like an old film run way too many times. In Athens, Connie and her husband Wayne helped heal us, their care and their friendship like a pair of hands lifting us up. The small chapel of Saint George at the top of Lykavitos Hill, the towering Acropolis—on those Athenian summits the penetrating, life-affirming light of Greece found its way around and into me. In that cauldron, the damp stranglehold of death and tears and incessant mourning was burned away. There were subsequent trips to Greece: to Madouri with poet and friend, Nanos Valaoritis; to Neaopoli; to Crete with Thanasis Maskaleris. "Come," he told us, his massive carnelian ring flashing as he took a deep drag from his Dunhill cigarette, "I'll prepare an island for you." Then a long hiatus...

My feet...the water laps up and touches my feet on the rocky beach in Aghios Ilias and I am thinking of Iphigenia. The water, which is jazz-blue, slaps the shore with a gentle smack, smack, smack. From my shady spot beneath a cowl of rock, I watch the women splashing about in it, breasts bobbing upon the cobalt surface. We have just dined on calamari at the small taverna above the beach. Calamari, *tzatziki*, Greek salad, eggplant salad, *spanakopita*—the meals are invariably similar, consistently delicious. Laughter bubbles up from the bodies playing in the surf. Crablike, I angle back toward the rock, protecting myself from the sun. I continue to puzzle over Iphigenia, whose story I chose to tell last night as we shared our favorite myths. I can't imagine why I chose this particular myth. Iphigenia, the ill-fated daughter of King Agamemnon and his queen, Clytemnestra, was sacrificed at Aulis so that the winds would blow, so that the Greek fleet could set forth to conquer Troy. It always struck me as so very sad that this poor child—she was a maiden, a *kore*—would become the sacrifice. In one version of the story (Euripides' play, I think) she is carried away by the wind. Yes, of course, there'd be a wind here. Carried off to the Black Sea where she is safe for a while.

In your bark beside the sleepy sea, close your eyes, my darling, wait for me.
There was a wind to carry Marissa off, wasn't there?

I like that version of the myth.

Iphigenia. The name haunts me. The women here talk about their daughters. Mary Jean's daughter is a poet and a dancer. Gail's daughter dances, as well. She'll be off to a new college this fall. Barbara's daughter, Piper, has just visited Neapoli. Together they hiked to Paradise. Doreen has a beautiful little granddaughter whose name is Kayla, a very wise little girl, according to Doreen, who gives Doreen so much pleasure. Linda Jue's two adopted daughters are from China. She shares their photos and details about their likes and dislikes. They have silky black hair and beautiful cheeks full of roses. I listened to these stories like an impoverished ghost. My girl is an invisible presence who sits silently beside me, follows me wherever I go. I wish I could point her out, share her with others. I am ashamed of my empty arms.

I've told only Virginia about my Iphigenia. "I had no idea why I selected that myth," I say, sitting in the front seat of her tiny car, and my eyes well with tears. This morning, heading off to her house from Connie's, where I'm staying, the cab driver—the drivers dance and sing here—rolled the windows of the car down, and Greece—the berry hills, the eye-blue sky—poured in. He had the radio on and the whine of the bouzouki, the tremolo of pipes was lifting me from my seat. The breeze had a song in it, too—an old one. The feeling, a melancholy ache fretted with joy, reminded me of my mother. The ghosts walk here. We keep wondering where the entrance to the underworld is. I have looked it up. Some say it is at Cape Tainaron on the Mani peninsula, the next knuckle of land on the Peloponnesian fist, that Odysseus and Heracles found their way into Hades' realm.

Others say the entrance is in Eregli, a city in Zonguldak Province, on the edge of the Black Sea. There are, I think, many entrances to the underworld, and there is surely one of them nearby, because my lost ones visit here. So palpable is their presence in this wind-tousled land. They are everywhere. I hear them in the spindrift whisper of the silver-leaves of olives; feel them in the silky webs the spiders cast across the little-traversed mountain paths we walk along; see their dark, mulberry messages written in the earth beneath those sacred trees. They are tied up in the sunlight and the wind and my own frangible carapace, the one that ticked off another birthday just before I left the United States.

One night Connie and Barbara celebrate for me with a chocolate cake, the filling between the layers thick with honey. There is dancing, laughter. Beautiful women, bejeweled and shawled, drift in and out of the parlor of Connie's home, out onto the terrace where the citronella burns, their laughter echoing down into the streets of Neapoli. "Invite the neighbors," says Connie, "that way you will have your party with no complaints." The neighbors are all there: Soula, Vassilis, Irene, and Lobbi, the editor of the local newspaper. We are eating squash blossoms stuffed with rice and cheese, eggplant, traditional *choriatiki* salad, drinking wine, and the young girls are dancing.

Connie's nieces, Chrysa and Alexa, on break from college and their whirlwind summer travels, are here to write as well. Chrysa, whose name means "golden blossom," looks as if she is dusted with the precious metal. Her hair falls about her shoulders in honey-colored curls; her eyes warm amber, almond-shaped. Her younger sister, Alexa, is like a princess, tall and fair, her dark hair cascading down her back in thick, black waves. "Come on, Linda, dance!" they command.

They are giving a lesson in Greek dancing. Behind them a growing tail of women snakes, weaving back and forth on the terrace between the chairs, the citronella candles, the occasional glass of wine. The moment is hypnotic. The women spread across the space like stars. I see constellations form, disassemble, form again, a tiny milky way of faces lit by party lights. And then my feet are moving to the rhythm, to Chrysa and Alexa's patient chant. The boisterous line of women winds around the small terrace. The girls call out the steps. I follow…

I sit in the hot, hot sun on one of Virginia's many terraces, listening to the stories, each one a beautiful creation. Mythic. Catherine's trip to the cemetery, Ann's interaction with the goddesses, Colleen's kiss, MJ's wild wind, Barbara's love affair with olives, Doreen's doctors and Dionysus, Gail's evil eye, Alexa's church, Chrysa's yiayia. Inside me there are stories forming also, but mine are so sad and confining.

When Thanasis comes I cling to him. He is quick to respond to my e-mail. I know he is in Greece. He is at a poets' and translators' conference in the House of Literature at the European Translation Center in Lefkes on the island of Paros where he is team-translating English texts into Greek and Greek into English. Will he, can he come here? He can lecture, I write, on Dionysus. Perhaps he answers me from Naxos where he claims he's gone to greet Ariadne. In the

myth about the labyrinth, Theseus abandoned her there. "Another
blow to the matriarchy," he says. Yes, he will come. He'll leave from
Tegea, in Arkadia, the region of his birth.

It's as though he has some kind of telepathy. Does he know
how much I need him? I am mourning, my sorrow deepening. I
am drifting further and further away. Thanasis is big and kind and
benevolent and as we sit in the taverna eating okra with tomatoes,
Greek salad and the little grilled fish, *barbounia*, eating even the heads,
I anchor on him. He is stalwart, a rock. Does he know as I hug him
that he is an island in the sea of my despair? Sometimes I can't
think. The stories crash around and inside me, wake me. Sometimes
they send me into dreams. I am lost in them, and when I surface
the wind assails me, grasshoppers surround me, the surf rasps like
a snare drum in the back of my mind. We are all, in some way, cast
adrift, I think. Together or not, we are always on our very separate
voyages, tossed on seas made entirely of our own experience. By day
we feel the sun, the breeze, the salt sea. In the evening the *korai* dance
and we drink wine and toast our travels...

In Faraklo, a small village nestled high up in the hills around
Neapoli where we are hiking one morning, Barbara shares what she
knows about the Greek concept of the *chorio*, the ancestral village.
It is the place from which one's family hails, the root, the heart of
a lineage, and the place to which future generations often return. I
have one, I know, somewhere in Japan. I have not been back, though
my brothers and my sister went there once as children, with my
mother, a few years before my younger brother, Paul, drowned in

the cold waters of the Trinity Alps. I have an ancestral village in Italy as well, and one in Wales where my grandfather was born. I have been to Japan, to Italy and to Wales, but always as a wanderer, a person without a home and I have not visited these family fonts. I wonder about them in a vague way, but I cannot bring myself to go. Perhaps one day I will. I don't know. I realize that it is not the familiar that draws me. I feel loose and rootless, roaming and meandering, an Odysseus of sorts, trying to find my Ithaka. Cavafy says Ithaka, the home base we seek, is ultimately within us, and that it is the search for Ithaka that inspires our travels.

Have Ithaka always in your mind;
to arrive there is what you are destined for.
But do not in the least hurry the journey.[1]

Once or twice I thought I had found it—Ithaka. Sometimes, for a little while, I find imaginary shelter in some cove, like here, in Vatika, but I am off again. There was a time when I believed there was a place where I could settle.

Ithaka gave you the beautiful voyage.
Without her you would have never set out.

But it's different now. I am on my own, and my daughter is gone, and there is nothing left but for the winds to blow.

---

[1] "Ithaka," Constantine Kavafis, translated by Tnanasis Maskaleris, *An Anthology of Modern Greek Poetry*, edited by Nanos Valaoritis and Thanasis Maskaleris, Talisman House, New Jersey, 2003.

About the Contributors

⤳

JOANNA BIGGAR is a teacher, writer and traveler whose special places of the heart include the California coast and the South of France. She has degrees in Chinese and French and, as a professional writer for twenty years, has written poetry, fiction, personal essays, features, news, and travel articles for hundreds of publications including *The Washington Post Magazine, Psychology Today, The International Herald Tribune,* and *The Wall Street Journal.* Her book *Travels and Other Poems* was published in 1996, and her most recent travel essays have appeared in Sportsfan.com and *Floating through France: Life Between Locks on the Canal du Midi.* She has taught journalism, creative writing, personal essay, and travel writing at The Writer's Center in Bethesda, Maryland since 1984, and "Spirit of Place" at the Writer's Center of Marin in San Rafael, California.

DIMITRI DELACOVIAS was born in Lachi, Vion, but grew up in Australia from the age of two. After several years as an illustrator and art director for advertising agencies in Sydney and then Athens, he moved to England in 1982 to work in television, where he joined the BBC in London as an assistant set designer. As digital technology started to take hold, he was one of the first people to work on the new Quantel digital paint box, which led to another change of career into the world of film visual effects. He currently works with one of the leading visual FX companies in London as senior Digital Matte Painter, where he has worked on such films *as The D'Vinci Code, World Trade Centre, Flyboys, Flight 93, Harry Potter 2, 3 & 4, The Chronicles of Riddick, AVP, Batman Begins, Kingdom of Heaven, James Bond, Below, Cold Mountain, Bridget Jones, Enemy at the Gates, Lost in Space* and *Seven Years in Tibet*. For the last four years he has taught the master class for Digital Matte Painting at Bournemouth University where he also is a guest lecturer on the subject. He has a house in Lachi which he tries to visit at least twice a year and is looking forward to retiring to his beloved Vatika in the very near future.

LINDA JUE was inspired by Watergate to become an investigative reporter nearly thirty years ago. Since then, she has, among other things, uncovered international political intrigue behind a local murder, exposed the politics of homelessness in San Francisco, documented the trends of Asian organized crime, and tracked down the fates of fleeing dissidents after Tiananmen Square. She has won several journalism awards. She currently directs a portfolio of national journalism programs as associate director of San Francisco-based Independent Press Association. She is a former associate of the Center for Investigative Reporting and a former editor at *San Francisco Focus* magazine. Her work has appeared in *San Francisco Focus*, the *San Francisco Bay Guardian, SF Weekly, GEO, Consumer Health Interactive, Los Angeles Times Syndicate, Toronto Globe and*

Mail, the former MacNeil/Lehrer NewsHour, PBS' Frontline, and other outlets. She also worked as the Northern California correspondent for C-SPAN. Linda is well known in the Bay Area media community for her involvement in media accountability and diversity issues. Her current work is part of a larger effort within the national media reform movement. When Linda isn't trying to save the world, she's busy just trying to live in it. She is prodded by a husband, two young daughters, and two Siberian hamsters.

THANASIS MASKALERIS was born in Arkadia, Greece and immigrated to the United States at the age of seventeen. He studied Philosophy and English at the University of Oklahoma, and Comparative Literature at Indiana University and UC Berkeley. He has written original poetry in Greek and in English, and has translated contemporary Greek poetry and prose extensively. He taught Classics, Comparative Literature and Creative Writing at San Francisco State University, until his recent retirement. He was Director of the Center for Modern Greek Studies from its founding in 1981 until 1996, and coordinated efforts that led to the establishment of the Nikos Kazantzakis Chair at SFSU. He recently co-translated, into English, Nikos Kazantzakis' *Russia*, and is currently working on a critical biographical study of Kazantzakis. During the past twenty years, he has frequently served on the Executive Committee of the Modern Greek Studies Association. His most recent publication (co-edited with Nanos Valaoritis) is *Modern Greek Poetry—An Anthology* (Talisman House Publishers, 2004).

COLLEEN K. MCFERRIN has straddled the business and artistic worlds for most of her life. Currently a realtor in the East Bay, Colleen began writing poetry and performing in shows, singing and dancing, as a very young girl. She studied classical voice and sang with the San Francisco Symphony Chorus and was a church soloist. She studied acting and has done some directing. She enjoys writing poetry and short stories and draws tremendous inspiration from traveling, being outdoors, gardening and relaxing with her husband Joe and two kitties, Bing and Crosby. Her story "The Italian Lesson" was published in *Hot Flashes: sexy little stories & poems.* "Corporate Connections" will be published this fall in a second *Hot Flashes* anthology. She is currently working on a children's book.

LINDA WATANABE MCFERRIN, poet, travel writer, novelist and teacher, is a contributor to numerous journals, newspapers, magazines, anthologies and online publications including the *San Francisco Examiner, The Washington Post, The San Francisco Chronicle Magazine, Modern Bride,* Travelers' Tales, Salon.com, and Women.com. She is the author of two poetry collections and the editor of the 4th edition of *Best Places Northern California.* A winner of the Nimrod International Journal Katherine Anne Porter Prize for Fiction, her work has also appeared in *Wild Places* and *American Fiction.* Her novel, *Namako: Sea Cucumber* was published by Coffee House Press and named Best Book for the Teen-Age by the New York Public Library. Her collection of award-winning short stories, *The Hand of Buddha,* was published in 2000. She is also co-editor of a prize-winning travel anthology and the recently released *Hot Flashes: sexy* *little stories & poems*. Linda has served as a judge for the San Francisco Literary Awards and the Kiriyama Prize. She holds an undergraduate degree in Comparative Literature and a Master of Arts degree in Creative Writing and is the founder of Left Coast Writers (http://leftcoastwriters.com). When she is not on the road, she directs art, consults on communications and product development, and teaches Creative Writing (www.lwmcferrin.com).

MARY JEAN PRAMIK, a coalminer's daughter and a great, great granddaughter of the Mongolian plain, has published copiously in medical journals, mined technical scientific metaphors, and launched three children. Mary Jean is the editor (a.k.a. ghostwriter) of the pharmaceutical thriller *Norethindrone; the First Three Decades,* available in most medical libraries, that relates the tortuous development of the first birth control pill. She has published in *Nature Biotechnology, Drug Topics,* and *Cosmetic Surgery News* as well as mainstream publications such as *Good Housekeeping* and the *National Enquirer.* Her poetry has appeared in college literary magazines and county fairs. She contributed to *Floating through France: Life Between Locks on the Canal du Midi.* Mary Jean lives in the San Francisco Bay Area where she moonlights as a political activist and fledgling triathlete. She is currently at work on a novel entitled *GEM of Egypt* and a book of essays, *Know It All.*

CATHERINE PYKE has worked for twenty years as a program officer for the Hearst Foundations in San Francisco, with headquarters in New York. Her work takes her to colleges and universities, medical centers and museums in urban and rural areas throughout the Western States. Frequent flights of imagination and long drives to reach programs in remote areas give her time to contemplate lives and places, which sometimes spark story ideas. She enjoys researching and writing about the lives of philanthropists, especially about the women who helped to shape higher education in California. A native of Salt Lake City, she currently lives in Larkspur, California. During her daily crossings by ferry to San Francisco, she delights in the beauty of the Bay.

GAIL STRICKLAND was hooked on writing from the moment her first short story was published in *Los Gatos High Literary Magazine*. Mom to Lara and Bram, step-mom to Stephen, Chris and Katie, surrogate mom to jazz musicians, dancers (friends of her own children) and the hundreds of piano students she adopted over the last forty-one years of teaching, she has recently written a novel, *Thalia*. Set in ancient Greece, it was inspired by her passion for Homer and her years of studying ancient Greek in college and living for several months on the island of Paros. With her youngest child starting college this year, Gail is simultaneously trying to publish completed works and finish a new novel, *Monasteries for the Mad*, about a young woman fleeing the "Dirty War" in Argentina. Gail lives in the San Francisco Bay Area with her husband Mike, a dog, a cat, a cockatiel, and a house full of books.

ALEXA TSAKOPOULOS is a sophomore at Columbia University. In addition to studying Columbia's core subjects, she is interested in studying writing, neurological science, and Greek Classics.

She is fluent in Spanish and looks forward to being fluent in Greek. She enjoys playing the accordion and listening to music by the Beatles. Among her friends she is known for her spastic dances and her ability to eat raw chocolate chip cookie dough. This is her first published work.

ANN KATHLEEN URE lives in the San Francisco Bay Area. By day, she directs a non-profit organization affiliated with apparel company Levi Strauss & Co. By night she dreams about becoming the next Erma Bombeck. Throughout her varied career she has written advertising copy, product fliers, song lyrics, grants, business proposals and first-person essays. Among her guilty pleasures she counts brunches with friends, hiking in Marin with her faithful dog, Sandy, crossword and sudoku puzzles, reality TV, karaoke, and harmonizing with anyone who can help her remember the lyrics to pop classics spanning the sixties to nineties. An essay about her 1994 bout with cancer was published by the Institute of Health & Healing at California Pacific Medical Center. In 2006, her travel stories were published in the anthology *Floating through France: Life Between Locks on the Canal du Midi* and in *France Today*.

DOREEN WOOD is a Canadian born writer who has either had a pen or keyboard in hand since she was a girl. As a medical rehabilitation professional, she has a repertoire of academic papers, grant writing, non-fiction personal essays and memoir. Doreen has completed a book entitled *Profoundly Ordinary*, stories of people who have survived a devastating disability. She also contributed to her husband's academic books. Whether it's writing stories about life with a disability, her own memoir, or personal essays, she writes with a keen eye to the emotional essence of a story, and maintains an incisive, yet fun-loving tone. She is also an avid traveler and her adventures give her food for thought and stories to weave. Story telling and exploring the intricacies of new people and places is a passion for her. Her northern Manitoba heritage, as in her taste for crisp French fries sizzling with sprays of pungent vinegar, is evident in many ways. Work on a memoir of her early years in Canada entitled *Sticks and Stones* is in progress.

ANNE WOODS has a degree in English from the University of the Pacific, where her parents sent her to study business or anything other than English. She knew she wanted to be a writer when she read Nevil Shute's novel *A Town Like Alice* in grade school. She has always imagined things in words. Anne grew up in a family of pilots and soloed a glider on her fourteenth birthday. She is a commercial pilot with Multiengine, Instrument, and Seaplane ratings. She has written for aviation publications and is a Certified Flight Instructor, mostly teaching people to fly right side up, although her preference is actually upside down. The lyrical grace of aerobatics, the unique view of the green and brown of a horizon inverted, have inspired her writing. An avid gardener and lover of waves crashing against reefs, Anne enjoys flying vintage airplanes with her husband and dreaming up stories about the people who might live in the towns she flies over.

CHRYSA TSAKOPOULOS is a third-year student at Georgetown University's School of Foreign Service in Washington D.C. studying International History. She is a native of Sacramento, California and loves to travel and teach English to children. Chrysa co-wrote the script and acted in the independent film *Mosaics* released in fall 2006. She enjoys reading poetry and historical novels, and loves dance of all types. She has participated in ethnic Greek dancing all her life and has recently fallen in love with tango. Her family is deeply involved in the promotion of Hellenism worldwide and has donated a comprehensive Hellenic library to California State University, Sacramento, and established chairs of Hellenic studies at a number of major universities. Her family has also contributed to the study of autism and founded the M.I.N.D. Institute at the University of California at Davis. Chrysa hopes to pursue a career in foreign policy. She is very proud to be a special supporter of *Venturing in Southern Greece: The Vatika Odysseys,* a travel book about her ancestral region of Vatika.

Index

About the Editors

BARBARA J. EUSER is a former political officer with the Foreign Service of the U.S. Department of State. As a director of the International Community Development Foundation, she has worked on projects in Bosnia, Somaliland, Zimbabwe, India and Nepal. At the end of the summer of 2005, she traveled to Greece to assess possibilities for a writing workshop. She fell in love with Vatika. Her articles and essays have appeared in magazines and anthologies. She is the  author of *Children of Dolpo*; *Somaliland*; *Take 'Em Along: Sharing the Wilderness with Your Children*; co-author of *A Climber's Climber: On the Trail with Carl Blaurock*; editor of *Bay Area Gardening*, *Gardening Among Friends* and *Floating through France: Life Between Locks on the Canal du Midi*. She lives near San Francisco with her husband. They have two grown daughters.

CONNIE BURKE left San Francisco, California in 1979. She set out for *Ithaka*, hoping to make her journey a long one, full of adventure, full of discovery. She has yet to return. On the way, she joined the English Faculty of the University of Maryland, European Division and The American College of Greece. Then she went on to establish and direct The Burke Institute for English Language Studies in Piraeus, Greece. Retired from  academia, Connie resides in Piraeus, where she serves as the first President of Habitat for Humanity, Greater Athens. When she is not hammering nails and cleaning paintbrushes, she spends her time reading, writing, and celebrating life in the southern Peloponnese.